Naamah

# Naamah

SARAH BLAKE

RIVERHEAD BOOKS
NEW YORK
2019

**RIVERHEAD BOOKS**
An imprint of Penguin Random House LLC
penguinrandomhouse.com

Library of Congress Cataloging-in-Publication Data

Names: Blake, Sarah (Poet), author.
Title: Naamah : a novel / Sarah Blake.
Description: New York : Riverhead Books, [2019]
Identifiers: LCCN 2018025679 (print) | LCCN 2018050436 (ebook) |
ISBN 9780525536352 (ebook) | ISBN 9780525536338 (hardback)
Subjects: LCSH: Noah's ark--Fiction. | Noah's wife (Biblical figure)--Fiction. |
BISAC: FICTION / Fairy Tales, Folk Tales, Legends & Mythology. |
FICTION / Literary. | FICTION / Religious. | GSAFD: Parables.
Classification: LCC PS3602.L3485 (ebook) | LCC PS3602.L3485 N33 2019 (print) |
DDC 813/.6--dc23
LC record available at https://lccn.loc.gov/2018025679

Printed in the United States of America
1  3  5  7  9  10  8  6  4  2

BOOK DESIGN BY LUCIA BERNARD

# Naamah

*And God saw that the wickedness of man was great in the earth.*

This may have been true. And if He'd told them that, they might have understood more. They might have learned that what ran through each of them, what they all felt, could in fact be named.

> *And the Lord said, I will destroy man whom I have created*
> *from the face of the earth.*

And while God would act harshly, He would not act impulsively. And between His deciding to destroy all things and the act of doing so, He came to know Noah.

> *Noah was a just man and perfect in his generations,*
> *and Noah walked with God.*
> *And Noah begat three sons, Shem, Ham, and Japheth.*

With Naamah. Naamah was the first one to know Noah to be a just man and perfect in his generations. Naamah married him before God ever spoke to him.

Naamah bore Japheth first. Then Shem. Then Ham. Though at some point Shem fell into the position of the baby of the family, spoiled and watched over. And Noah's walks with God continued, every afternoon, and sometimes into the night, as Naamah raised the boys.

When Noah brought home God's command to build the ark, Naamah helped him to make a model of the ark out of stalks of grass. "How can we do this?" Noah asked. And though neither of them could answer, they began the work of it.

> *And every thing that is in the earth shall die.*
> *But with thee will I establish my covenant.*

They hurried their boys to marry, and they did without difficulty. Japheth married Adata; Ham, Neela; Shem, Sadie. Then there were eight of them to build. They worked for years. At night, they left and ate with their families, they played with children in the dirt. It was impossible for them to envision the destruction of the world. And why should they?

Noah and Naamah shook with their imaginings.

> *Two of every sort shall come unto thee, to keep them alive.*

"How can we do this?" Noah asked Naamah again.

"If we don't, we'll die," she answered. They were sitting on their bed.

"Maybe we should die," he said, "if every one of us is wicked."

"No," she said, and she took him in her arms because he had begun to cry. "If I am sure of anything, I am sure that you and our children should not die."

He did not say anything.

"I need you to be sure of it, too, Noah." She pushed him away from herself. "I need for you, when you look at me, to be overwhelmed with the feeling that I should not die."

He looked at her and nodded slowly.

"You don't feel it," she said.

"I want to."

"What about our sons? Do you want them to die?"

He shook his head.

"But you think that maybe they should?"

He nodded and she stormed around their bed, keeping her eyes up so he could see how she did not look at him.

"Is it not love?" he shouted at her.

She stopped and put her face very close to his. "Love is protecting them."

Neither of them said anything for a long time. They stayed in that position as if she could pin the thought into his head with her eyes.

"Are you with me?" he asked her.

"I am always with you," she said.

> *And Noah went in, and his sons, and his wife,*
> *and his sons' wives with him, into the ark.*

When the rains began, Noah's doubt left him.

When the rains continued, his guilt left him.

When the waters were high enough to lift the ark from the earth, he and all the family were asleep.

When they woke, they were adrift.

And what was remarkable, to them all, was that they could not feel the difference between the earth covered with life and the earth barren of it. They each had thought they'd feel it somewhere in their bodies—their chest or gut or bones—but none of them did.

*And the waters prevailed upon the earth.*

There was a time, then, when God forgot about the ark on the floodwaters. It was not a long time for God, but it was a long time. Enough that the family began to feel as if they had always been adrift. The waking to water, every day, flat and blue and everywhere. When someone dies and you forget how they look or how they laughed, that is how they forgot the land.

But only Naamah mourned it. The rest of them were merely eager to see it again.

Naamah sometimes imagined the water was land. That she could stand on it and face the boat, which she refused to call an ark anymore, disenchanted with it and these weeks with the animals, rowdy and foul.

From the surface of the water, the side of the boat seemed insurmountable, too big to be real. But given time and tools, she thought, she could climb it. She could solve it.

Naamah knew that the true difficulty was in her own position, on the boat.

# ONE

Naamah is watching the horizon, hoping something will interrupt it and distract her, pull her eye to it, a moment of focus. She is humbled by the flood, but how long can someone reasonably be asked to experience humility?

She hears Noah's steps behind her and turns to him. "You scared me," she says.

"Sorry. I came to find you."

If she positioned Noah just right, along the railing, if she backed away from him, maybe his dark body would be tall enough to break the horizon. "I don't feel well," she says.

"Sick?" He puts his arms around her waist.

There are chickens and other animals wandering the deck. She can hear them, but she can't see them.

"No," she says. "Tired."

"Go tend to an animal."

She sways her body in a loose *no*.

"Let one nuzzle into your hand."

He's right. That used to cheer her up. "I can't see them anymore," she admits.

"You can't see them?" He comes around beside her, looks at her.

"No," she says. She states it so plainly she surprises herself.

The chickens are around their feet now, knowing Noah often has grain in his pocket. She feels one brush her leg and her body jumps; she hadn't realized how close they were. She doesn't know why she can't see them, but she's almost happy to be free of them, in this one way.

"Maybe you'll be able to see them again tomorrow," Noah says.

But that makes her feel worse. She squeezes her eyes shut.

Noah puts his hand on hers. "Come to bed, won't you?"

"It smells down there," she says.

"Then we'll sleep up here tonight. I'll get blankets."

"Okay," she agrees, and he is already off with purpose in his quick step.


SLEEPING ON THE DECK IS COLD, even under the blankets and folded into Noah, against his large, flat stomach. She remembers nights in the desert, in the tent, sleeping in this same position, but warm. They started so near to home; now, she can't say where they are. She thinks that air must get cooler as it crosses the water. She thinks of the air traveling with such freedom across the earth, and she falls asleep.


HER OLDEST SON, Japheth, often stands with her, looking out over the water. He's not much taller than she is. She doesn't have to raise her head to look him in the eye when he speaks. He tries to keep conversation light, tries to keep her happy, as if her unease depends on whether he can make her laugh. But sometimes he lets her lead the conversation where she'd like.

"Do you think about how many animals died?" she asks.

"Yeah."

"Do you think about how many people died?"

"Yeah, Mom."

"Do you think about the little things? Like what clothes they were wearing?"

"No."

"Only the big things."

"Yeah."

"Like how terrible it would be to drown?"

"Yeah."

She turns even further to the water. "It's all I can think about." She opens her shoulders to the floodwaters, which she wants to call *the sea*. "When do you think it will go down?"

"Soon. I have to think it's soon."

"Yes," Naamah says.


HER FIRST LABOR, with Japheth, had been the most difficult. She had cramps through the night, then the mucus fell out, bloody and thick, then the pain, then the water, then, eventually, Japheth. They saw his head so many times, with each push, before she could get him out. But she did. And then her next sons came easily, as if Japheth had broken something that never needed to be set right again.

When Japheth was a teenager, he noticed that one of his teeth still had a ragged top, as all his teeth had when they first tore through his gums. He ran his fingernail over it again and again. It made a small click only he could hear. He asked Naamah if it would ever flatten, but she didn't know.

As soon as she birthed him, she knew that his body would be the most unpredictable thing in her life. It should have been obvious. Noah's body was not hers. No one's body was hers but her own. But after growing Japheth, after seeing the shape of his head through her skin, she felt deeply that his body *was* hers. And that feeling never passed. Later, as she had her other sons, the feeling grew less distinct and gave the illusion of passing, but then something would happen— say, a skin tag growing at an alarming rate near the crease of his elbow—and she would feel it again. How he belonged to her. And how separate they were.

She also began to feel separate from her own body. During that first labor, she had developed a hemorrhoid, which she didn't notice until weeks later, when it was no longer filled with blood, just a fold of skin that refused to retreat. If she gathered it up and pushed it down, it felt like a soft, round button. Otherwise it sagged. Her body made less and less sense to her as it seemed to reject itself.

But she loved to think of that first labor, holding on to that memory more vividly than others, than normal, happy times, eating dinner, playing games with the boys, telling them stories. She wanted to remember those times, but what could she do? Now she revisits her body in full contraction, covered in sweat. She can see the color of the sand beside her. She can feel the desert air rush through the tent, opened in the back and front, to cool her. She can no longer smell it, but the rest is enough.

NAAMAH LAYS OUT LUNCH on a blanket on the deck. Bowls of hummus, flatbread, dried figs, water to pass around. Noah and Japheth come to the deck first, followed by the younger sons, Shem and Ham, and then each of her sons' wives, as if they'd been speaking somewhere, privately.

"Good morning," Noah says, beaming at his children.

They all say their good mornings, first to Noah and then to each other, nodding little nods, smiling, sitting down in spots that have become theirs in the weeks since the rains stopped.

They eat quietly. They seem to pause to smell the wind off the sea, but it is not the sea; the smell is not salty but cool and crisp and not unpleasant.

Shem shoos away two goats that Naamah cannot see. Ham's wife, Neela, tosses a bit of bread in their direction. Naamah watches the bread land, then watches it disappear. She can picture the animal so clearly: its bent neck, its lips and teeth. She doesn't need to see it.

"Don't do that," Naamah says.

Neela looks embarrassed until Ham places his hand on her hand, and Neela remembers she doesn't need to mind Naamah.

FOR FORTY DAYS AND FORTY NIGHTS, they had to stay below deck. One time, Naamah undressed and snuck up. The rain hurt her skin as it fell on her, as she watched it beat the deck and then rush off the sides through the bars of the railing. The boat rocked, but not enough to worry her, just enough to let the water show how it could move together, just enough that one could imagine how waves form.

When she couldn't take it any longer, she returned to her room with Noah, her brown skin beaten pink. Noah rushed to her with a blanket and held her, dried her, warmed her, and she hid how much it hurt her, to be held then. The next day it was easy enough to avoid anyone's touch. And the day after that her skin had calmed.

She had wanted to try going out again, to test the feeling, but she was overwhelmed by her new understanding of the deaths of the people God no longer wanted.

Now, AFTER LUNCH, Naamah sits on the deck with a mallet and chisel, some rope, and a piece of wood, slightly longer than the width of her. She hammers holes into the wood and threads the rope through. Once the rope is in place, running along the underside of the wood and splaying out of the other side like two tentacles, she sits down on the wood and pulls the ends of the rope up around herself.

She raises her arms above her head, trying to imagine the safest way to position the rope if she were deadweight. She lets herself slowly feel out the differences in the rope, higher and lower, with her head hung and with it raised. The rope is rough and reminds her of a braid of hair.

When everything feels right, she readjusts the lengths of rope on either side of her and ties a square knot, securing it. She tests it again, her hands above her, her head leaning into the softness of her own upper arm.

She's so near to completing the swing that she fills with excitement. She has been building it in her mind for days and has to remind herself not to rush now.

Finally, she adds another rope to the end of her first with a sheet bend knot. She uses two half hitches to tie it to the railing by the stairs. In her eagerness, she pulls on it harder than necessary, to make sure it holds. Her hands are burned. Where they were already chapped, they bleed.

Blood marks the wood of the seat when she grabs it and throws it over the side. She closes her eyes to listen, to hear if the rope is long enough to reach the water. It is. She hears it splash. She takes a few deep breaths, reveling in this small glory. Then she pulls the seat back up, leaves it to mark the deck a shade darker with its wetness, for as long as the sun will allow.

WHEN THE BOYS WERE YOUNG, they would walk quite far to the river for water. The boys would get their feet wet in the shallows and run away from the muddy bank, as fast as they could, hoping their feet would stay wet long enough to make footprints when they reached the sand. Shem's small feet were somehow always dry when he got there; Ham left only heel prints because he'd run on tiptoe through the softer dirt. Japheth teased them both.

Naamah caught Shem looking at the bottoms of his feet as if something were wrong with them. She took off her shirt, wet it in the river, and laid it down. Ham immediately stepped on the shirt and made a detailed footprint, but Shem looked at her for permission. She nodded him on. He jumped on the shirt and then jumped away, leaving two perfect little feet staring back at them in the sand.

NAAMAH RUNS THROUGH the lower deck, calling for Noah. She passes the wives in a room, laughing about something. Sometimes they bring a small animal into a room, say a chinchilla, and laugh at its behaviors, sharing the story with the family later over dinner, cooing, *How adorable.* Naamah has no time for them.

"Noah!"

She passes more doors. By now, even though she can't see the animals, she knows where each of them rests. They used to make a lot more noise than they do now, and while she is glad for the relief, she worries they've grown accustomed to the boat. That makes her feel sick.

"Noah!"

Noah comes around a corner with a concerned look on his face; she's going so quickly that she runs into him. She laughs, and that catches him off guard and puts him at ease at the same time.

"What is it?" he says.

"Come with me." She would grab his hand but the halls are too narrow for that. She leads him to the deck, where the swing is. She undresses quickly. He smiles but doesn't understand until it's too late, until he sees her jump over the side of the boat.

"Naamah!" he shouts after her, and he immediately starts undressing, his eyes fixed on the water. His shirt is off when she resurfaces, spitting and splashing.

"Are you okay?" he shouts.

"Yes!" she yells back. She looks up and she's smiling. "When I'm done swimming, throw down the swing!"

"Are you done *now*?" Even yelling, she can hear the worry mixed into the joke.

"No! No, let me enjoy this!"

"It's not too cold?"

"I'm fine!"

She starts to follow the length of the boat, swimming on her side, but the boat is too long. Her breath tires first. Then her arms. She has to stop and float on her back, but this view of the sky is different, obscured by the boat, shaded but still lit, blue.

WHEN SHE NO LONGER wanted to go out in the flood's rain, she'd still come to the trapdoor that led to the deck and listen to it falling on the boat.

She had heard stories of light rains, of rains that pitter-pattered, that sprang lightly, but she was used to desert rains that came on fast and left everything drenched. She thought the flood rains would be like that, too. But they weren't. Their sound was horrible and flat in its constancy.

If she had to describe it, she would recall how each of her sons had, at some point, discovered that if they peed on a rock, the pee would splash. They would pee as hard as they could, aiming at an ant or a leaf, until their legs were covered in a spray of their own pee.

The rain reminded her of that, except that the rain came in a million streams. Which made her imagine God as a being with a million penises. Which terrified her. But she feared that He would see her terror and punish her for it, so she tried to feel love, instead, for the many-penised creature inside her head.

SHE HEARS THE swing slapping the side of the boat.

"Naamah, come back up! Please!"

Naamah swims over to the swing, grabs the rope, pulls herself up, swings her legs through, and seats herself on the wood. She positions herself exactly as she'd planned, but it feels different this way, her legs hanging heavy over the wood.

"Ready," she calls up to him.

As he starts to pull, she uses the balls of her feet to bounce up the boat. Otherwise her body would be scraped against it. The boat would lick her coarse.

WHEN NOAH AND NAAMAH had gone looking for a place in the desert to build the ark, they found a trove of cypress trees that God had made for them. They cut down one and fashioned a giant tub and a small bucket. They collected sap in the small bucket, from every tree, and gathered it all in the tub. Then they began to cut down the small forest.

As the boys grew strong, as they married, as the family grew, everyone worked. Shem's wife, Sadie, cried often in the first days. Naamah once overheard her asking Shem why her family, her young sisters and brothers, could not come with them. Shem did not respond. Naamah walked over to Sadie and held her tight. As Sadie began to sob, Shem snuck out, his eyes red and ready to weep. When Sadie's sobs turned into soft hiccups, Naamah stood her up.

"That was the last time you can cry about this."

And Sadie looked as if it all might begin again.


As NAAMAH CLIMBS BACK onto the boat, over the railing, Noah groans. And when she is steady on the deck, Noah looks her over to make sure no harm has come to her. Then he says, "I'm not a young man, Naamah."

"Next time I'll ask the boys to pull me up."

"No. It's not safe. I don't think."

"I think it is." She starts to get dressed again.

"Can't we just . . . get through this?"

"That," she says, standing up straight, "is exactly what I am trying to do."


AFTER ALL THE TREES WERE CUT, prepared, sawn into thousands of pale planks, they started to build. The work exhausted them all. They ate between shifts, quickly, to fill a need. They drank water that way, too, draining cups in one long draft. At night, they all fell asleep without a word.

Naamah made more buckets with Sadie and Neela. They collected rabbit shit. They made fires and fished burnt sticks out of the flames for charcoal, preparing to turn the sap to pitch. Once the boat was finished, they would have to work fast, covering the planks while the pitch was still warm, while the sun was high.

Japheth's wife, Adata, helped the men with the boat. She was better than all the others at visualizing how the boat must be at the end, how that end would grow out of the small parts they could accomplish each day.

NAAMAH SWIMS EVERY AFTERNOON, when the water is warm but the sun is hidden behind one side of the boat, so she can swim and float on her back without the sun ever catching her eye in that piercing way that reminds her of God's reach.

Stronger and faster, Naamah decides to dive below the water. She goes as far as she can without opening her eyes, just stretching her arm out ahead of her, but she finds nothing. She thinks of the water as an emptiness, and when the thought strikes her she recoils, her hand jerking back toward her stomach. The water's thick resistance brings the reality back to her. *It is a thing. It is not a void.*

She dives again, but not as far, and this time she opens her eyes. At first she can't make anything out. Then her eyes adjust as they would in a dark room. It's difficult to keep from floating up, so she moves forward instead. Soon, beyond her, and lower, farther down, she sees a tree. Its form, at ease in the water. Its form, spectacularly large.

THAT NIGHT, after too many restless nights on the boat, Naamah finally sleeps soundly again. She dreams of the tree covered in leaves, as if it had been able to hold on to them through the rains. The leaves wave like a school of fish, only much more slowly. Her body, in the dream, is no longer slow. Without the water's resistance, she reaches the tree. The leaves are soft. She slips between the branches. She looks up toward the surface. The water looks the same in all directions—she is surrounded by a million dark circles waiting for her to discover them, to point her aquiline nose toward them, to give her the illusion of a focused center.

The water shifts, and the leaves close her off like an eye.

THE NEXT DAY, Naamah swims again. Her sons stand around on the deck, waiting to pull her up. The blocks of sun climb Shem's legs where he stands.

"I touched a tiger last night," he says.

"No, you didn't," Japheth responds, without even pausing to consider it.

"I did. Seriously. It was near the door, and I slid my fingers underneath and felt its fur."

"What was it like?" Ham asks.

"I don't know. What you'd expect. Soft." He looks down and sees a corner of sun sitting neatly on his calf.

"Then why do it?" Japheth asks.

"I don't know. To say I touched a tiger." He smiles at Japheth, and Japheth can't help but smile back at his young fool of a brother.

IN THE WATER, Naamah tries diving again. She wants to see the tree, but it's not there. The boat must have moved; it's always moving, in its own inconstant way.

She's about to come back up for air when she sees a woman. She's far off, near formless, but enough form to show she's a woman. And whoever she is, she has noticed Naamah, and she is fleeing. Naamah tries to follow her, but she doesn't make it far. She's already been under for too long.

WHEN SHE REACHES THE SURFACE, she hears Ham calling for her. He sounds scared. She wants to go back under, to find the woman, but she hesitates. She treads water, catching her breath.

"There she is! Mom!" Shem calls out.

"Over here!" Ham calls, but angry now instead of scared, as if she's betrayed him.

She looks toward them. She is farther out than she's ever been.

"Can you make it back to the ark?" Japheth yells.

She nods. She slips under again to slick her hair back, to feel closer to the woman.

"Mom, come back!" Ham again.

She makes an effort toward the boat.

"WHAT WERE YOU DOING OUT THERE?" Noah asks her, back in the quiet of their room, if you can call a boat filled with animals quiet.

"I thought I saw something."

"What?"

She shrugs.

"What?"

"A woman." She looks away from him. "I thought I saw a woman."

"A dead woman?"

She looks back, surprised. "No. A swimming, alive woman."

He's never quick to respond to anything. He's always thoughtful. Now is no different.

Naamah asks, "Do you think there are dead women down there?"

"Yes."

"I thought maybe He'd cleared them away somehow."

"Maybe He has. I don't know."

"Is that why you didn't want me swimming?"

"Yes." He touches her wet hair. "I'm sorry—I thought that was obvious."

"I hadn't thought of it." She takes in a little breath and releases it. "It feels freeing, to swim, to be part of the flood. We've been so separate from it, from everything."

"But we are together."

"I feel a boundary around us, around every pair of animals here. Like we're carting around a hundred planets."

"Isn't that a good thing?"

"I don't know. Planets are heavy. I feel like we should have sunk. Why haven't we sunk?"

"You know why."

"I don't!" she yells, trying to get him to yell, too.

He takes a few deep breaths, and she watches his chest take them. It calms them both.

"Yes, you do," he says.

"Yes, I do," she says.

The boat rocks them slightly, enough so they know they are on water, but not enough to displace anything in the room. She's complicit again.

# TWO

Before they started to build the boat, Naamah had become close to a widow, Bethel, who lived nearby. Naamah had heard that Bethel knew where to find berries, so the first time they met they went off together to find some. Bethel's sure steps led the way, and Naamah was attuned to the shifts of Bethel's body leading them in one direction and then another.

Naamah had expected to find only enough berries for each of her children to have a taste. Instead the women found a flurry of bushes, filled with berries in such surplus that Naamah felt sure they were a gift from God. They sat and stuffed themselves, told each other stories of their long lives, sat quietly and watched bees search the bushes for the blossoms that were there before the fruits matured.

The next day Bethel found a reason to visit Naamah, showing up at her tent. Naamah remembers her standing there, her graying hair in a loose twist down her back. Soon they saw each other every day. At first they took walks and did errands together, but then they started staying in. And before long they were lying together in Bethel's tent, in Bethel's bed.

No one bothered a widow with her tent closed in the heat.

Naamah and Bethel could hear children playing outside. Naamah thought this would make her uncomfortable or embarrassed, but the sounds of children carrying on reminded her that she was in a place she loved, a place full of joy. Looking at Bethel, she thought of how she'd lived through so many stages of her life—childhood, adulthood, motherhood. She was owed a stage she could not name.

Every day that Naamah came into the tent, Bethel tied it shut behind her. She undid Naamah's hair and undressed her and then undressed herself. They lay on the bed and held each other so close their faces were beside each other, Bethel's slightly higher. Naamah didn't know if Bethel kept her eyes open or closed as she ran her hand up and down Naamah's back. Sometimes she ran her hand down over her butt and sometimes up over her shoulder and around to her upper arm, and the interruption to the pattern of movement sent chills over Naamah's body. Sometimes Naamah fell asleep and Bethel let her. Sometimes they kissed. Sometimes Naamah couldn't stand it and she grabbed Bethel's hand and moved it to her vulva, where Bethel would hold her steady until Naamah's arm relaxed again and Bethel began to move her fingers in circles that swept the quickening wetness at her opening up to the tip of her clitoris until everything was wet and Naamah was moaning through her bit lip.

When she was young, Naamah had needed Noah's full force inside her to reach the top of what her body was capable of reaching. Sex left her exhausted and energized at once. As she got older, her orgasms could be quiet, soft. She could fall asleep afterward, the way Noah always had. And if they weren't having sex often enough, she would have orgasms in her sleep. She needed merely to dream of kissing Noah, pressing into him with her hips, to have an orgasm that would leave her sated for days, weeks sometimes. But orgasms with Bethel were better than anything she could dream up.

Naamah would try to match what Bethel had done for her, and while Bethel did not make any noise, her whole body shook. Naamah felt like Bethel could shake fruit from a tree, the way her body's shaking came in regular intervals. Naamah would try to kiss her neck and Bethel would push her away, hold her there, taking slow, measured breaths. When Bethel thought her body had settled, she'd pull Naamah back, kiss her, and when she would shake again, they would laugh.

Noah didn't notice all the afternoons Naamah spent in Bethel's tent because his days were full, spent talking with God.

NAAMAH STARTS SWIMMING as often as she can make an excuse to go. And under the water, it happens again and again. She spots the woman, and the woman spots her, and the woman swims away before Naamah can learn anything new about her. Naamah returns to the surface out of breath and slaps the water in frustration. And her frustration follows her back onto the boat.

The boys pull her up and leave her to dress again, talking among themselves. She dresses quickly and heads down to her room. But as she nears her door, she has another idea. She goes down another deck, and then down again, to the boat's lowest deck. It's cold. She wonders if she's now farther below the surface than she's been able to dive. She's always looked away from the boat when she's dived, never thinking to look back, never wanting to.

Here, among the rooms of animals who prefer the cold, Naamah tends a smaller room, one where she's stored all the seeds she could collect and dry. Inside it, the room is dark and cool, and it feels good at first. But then she starts to feel how warm and damp she is, like an obtrusion, a risk to all the future plants of the earth.

She clatters out of the room, slams the door behind her. She hears a bear snuff through its nostrils. She starts to walk down the long hallway back to the stairs, but she hears more animals shuffle around, as if they can sense her at each door she passes.

At one door, she hears a loud smash by her ear. Splinters of wood hit her on the arm and cheek. She can't tell which was first, the impact of the wood or the sound of it. Everything is out of order in her head. She stares at the door, the new, long hole in it, broken by something unseen.

*Walrus*, she thinks. *This is where the walrus are.* A walrus has swung its giant tusk downward, toward her, through the door, and as Naamah puts that together, she runs. As she reaches the stairs, though, the shuffling of the animals stops, and she pauses. All she can hear is her own panting breath and the crying of the bearer of the tusk. She walks back toward the door. She cannot see the tusk, but she can picture it, large and yellowed, almost part of the door now, stuck and still.

Still panting from the scare, she leans on the wall across from the broken door, tries to convince her body that she is at rest as she listens to the trapped walrus whimper. Soon the walrus's mate begins to whimper as well.

Naamah steadies herself and approaches the door, her hand raised and open until she can feel the tusk, hard and rougher than she thought it would be. For a moment, the walrus startles. She tries to imagine breathing in a bright light and breathing it out again through her hand and into the tusk. She runs her other hand to the bottom of the tusk, and uses both hands to push gently up. Not that she has the strength to move it. Only to suggest to the walrus that moving it in that direction might free it.

Naamah hears the walrus shake, the grunt of effort, the creak of wood. And the tusk is free. The walrus and Naamah both back away from the door, and finally she runs to get someone to help her mend it, unsure of whether the walrus understands the weakness of the door, if the walrus would charge it, given the chance.

OUT IN THE DESERT, when the pitch was ready, Naamah dipped a bucket into it. They would need a sealed bucket to shit in, to clean up with, and she knew no one else would think of this.

She covered five buckets in all, and hung them on a branch to dry. She laid out a tarp beneath them to catch any black drops, until she remembered the coming flood. The earth hardly needed protection from such a small offense. Still, she felt sorry for the ground beneath her, so she lay down and apologized to it. The buckets hung above, like heads in the tree. The image would haunt her for months, almost any time she closed her eyes.

NAAMAH SITS AT THE END of the hallway as Japheth and Adata mend the door. "The animals are uneasy," she says.

Japheth and Adata agree.

"What can we do?"

"I don't know, Mom." Japheth leans against the door and looks at her. "We try to keep them moving. We run them around the deck, the ones we can. We check in on them. We feed them. We clean up after them."

She knows. She knows they clean up more of their shit than seems possible, coaxing them into an adjoining room to feed them while their room is cleaned, then switching them back again, so one room always smells of shit and one of blood.

She also knows that cleaning up after them means stealing litters of babies that have come too soon, before any land can be seen. Mostly the babies are fed to other animals, but sometimes a mother eats her own young. Once, when Naamah could still see the animals, she was so tired that she threw a litter of eight mice overboard instead of finding a more useful place for them to die. It was her job then to deal with the young. Now it's Noah's. Neither of them can bring themselves to make the children do it.

"I've heard Sadie sing to them," Adata says, not looking up from her work, inspecting the door, wondering if they should replace it entirely.

Naamah didn't know that. "What does she sing to them?"

"Lullabies."

AS WORK ON THE BOAT PICKED UP, Naamah sat down with her sons and their new wives.

"You cannot have sex on the boat," she said.

They were silent. The women had not had time yet to get to know Naamah. They'd thought she was sitting them down to welcome them to the family, formally, or at least warmly. Her sons knew better.

"This is not to say you shouldn't enjoy each other," she went on. "You just cannot have sex." Naamah continued, in case they didn't understand. "We don't know how long the waters will last, and we can't afford to have a pregnancy in that—"

"We get it," Adata said.

"Good." Naamah looked to her sons, who nodded. "Good," she repeated, looking to Sadie and Neela. They kept their eyes down. Naamah decided it was best to leave them to discuss it among themselves.

"WHAT WAS SEX LIKE with your husband?" Naamah asked Bethel.

"He liked to hold up my legs, and sit straight up while I was lying down. He liked it because he could watch my breasts bounce. I watched him sometimes, but mostly I kept my eyes closed. Sometimes we would wake in the night and both want to have sex, and I would raise my leg slightly, turn open my hips, so he could go in from behind and we'd hardly have to move. That might have been my favorite."

"Really your favorite, or only because it was a rare occasion?"

"I don't know. I think really my favorite."

"Have you ever had sex standing up?" Naamah asked.

"No. But I've always wanted to."

"We could do it."

"No, I think I've always wanted to with a man," Bethel said.

Naamah shouldn't have felt rejected in that moment, but she did.

———————

LATE ONE NIGHT, Naamah passes Ham and Neela's room and hears them having sex. Neela is moaning, and there is a rhythmic thudding that doesn't come from anything else.

Naamah finds Noah on the deck. He is holding a pole with a looped rope on one end, hanging, suspended. He is running an animal. He lets the animal lead him around the deck, but always keeping his strength in his arms, a tension against the pole.

"What do you have there?" Naamah asks.

"A wolf," he says.

"Can you stand still with her for a second?"

"Him. And sure."

Noah stands and turns on a pivot as the wolf makes his way in a loop around him.

"Neela and Ham are having sex."

"Do you think we need to do something about that?"

"I know we can't handle a pregnant woman right now, on top of everything else."

"No, but maybe he's pulling out."

"You know that doesn't always work."

"I know," Noah says, "but how much longer will we even be on the ark?"

"I don't know."

"And maybe it would be nice to have a child around?"

"Nice?"

"Naamah, come on."

"Nice for who? Not for the child. To grow up here."

"No child would grow up here. It would just be for a time. A time a child wouldn't even remember."

"We don't know that," Naamah says.

"We don't, but they're adults. They have to do what they need to."

"You better not talk like this around them. We'll end up with three pregnant women."

"I won't," Noah says.

She looks at the end of the pole, wonders which direction the wolf is looking.

"I promise I won't," he says again.

"What's the wolf doing?" she asks.

Just then the far end of the pole drops down to the deck, making a faint tap they both hear.

"Naamah!" Noah screams.

By instinct she raises her arms, crosses them in front of herself. The wolf leaps, going for her throat. She manages to block him with her arms, but the force of his jump pushes her back, over the railing, and she crashes into the water.


NOAH STOMPS ON THE DECK and yells and yells. Shem hears first and starts shouting, too, as he runs to the deck. Soon the whole boat is a mess of animal noises. Even the wolf is scared. Noah makes himself large and boxes the wolf into a corner.

"Grab the net," Noah yells to Shem, keeping his eyes trained on the wolf's eyes.

Japheth and Ham are there now, and they help Shem get the net over the wolf, fold him up in it, and get him on his side.

"Take him back down to his room, Japheth," Noah says.

Japheth nods and drags the limp wolf along the deck.

Noah rushes over to the side of the boat, which is still shaking with every startled animal. "And calm those animals down!"

"What happened, Dad?" asks Ham.

"I got distracted and the damn thing chewed the rope off the stick."

"That doesn't sound so unusual."

"It lunged at your mother."

At the same instant, the boys figure it out. "Where is she, Dad?" asks Shem.

"Why haven't you gone in after her yet?" Ham yells, his voice cracking.

"I would!" Noah shouts, scanning the water. "I mean I will. But I can't tell where she is."

All of them are looking in the water now.

"Can you see her?" he asks them.


NAAMAH FEELS A PAIN burst through her hips and shoulders, from one side of her body to the other, as she crashes into the water. Blood is spilling out of the gash on her arm from the teeth of the wolf. Her clothes rise over her body and she knows she is falling deeper. When her clothes settle, she has trouble telling which way is up.

This is when the woman comes to her, the one she has seen before.

"You are safe," she says.

Naamah's eyes scramble over her black skin.

"You can speak here."

Naamah opens her mouth and the water does not come into it. She closes it again.

The woman waits.

Naamah moves her mouth more slowly. She can feel there a kind of film, which she seems to create with the parting of her lips. She touches her fingers to her open mouth. It feels like the film that forms on top of partly churned milk—what people call skin, though it's hard to imagine skin without the firmness of the body beneath it. This is a weightless skin. This is impossible.

She spots the blood still leaving her arm in trails like a hair's curl, as if she might fondle it. "Am I okay?" she asks.

"Yes."

"Will I be?"

She nods.

"What now?" Naamah asks.

"I bring you back to the ark."

"You know about the boat?"

She nods.

"Who are you?"

"I am an angel of the Lord."

"Shit." Naamah's eyes scramble again. "Shit. Shit. Shit."

"You have nothing to fear, Naamah."

"Nothing to fear? I have everything to fear! What are you doing down here?"

The angel doesn't respond.

Naamah knows what it could be. "You are cleaning up the dead."

The angel shakes her head.

"You are hiding the massacre."

"No."

"Where are the dead, then?" Naamah spots a tree and swims toward it, uses it to orient herself, swims down. Her ears begin to hurt.

The angel follows her patiently. "Here, let me help with that." She touches Naamah and Naamah's ears stop hurting and she gains a sort of gravity in the water.

"Where did they go?" Naamah asks.

"Do you have no other questions?"

Naamah stops, calms herself. She can tell the angel is beautiful, but she can't describe her. The angel flickers in and out of focus like any object in the water, but this seems more calculated, as if to mislead Naamah, so that she might sound mad if she ever tried to describe her to anyone. She searches for some detail about her to hold on to—the color of her eyes, a scar, anything.

"Are you here to judge me?" Naamah asks.

"No."

"Do you regret me as He does?"

"He does not regret you."

"He does not regret Noah. I am just loved by the man He does not regret."

"Is that not enough?"

"No," Naamah says, "that is not enough."

The angel says nothing.

"Do you regret me?" Naamah asks again.

"I don't know yet."

"But you will stay to find out, won't you?"

And then Naamah is in Noah's arms, choking and coughing as he pulls her backward, through the water, toward the swing.

## THREE

Naamah doesn't swim again for days. Her family doesn't want her to, of course, but she doesn't want to either. She is quiet at meals. Ever since she's been back on the boat, she can see the animals again. Perhaps she was close to death, she thinks; perhaps she's been reborn in some way. Or maybe her restored vision is a gift from the angel, to keep Naamah from getting herself killed on the boat. Whatever the cause, it brings her no happiness. She sees nothing but hooves that need trimming, nails that need clipping, flaking skin in their fur. Every sight a chore to be done.

She starts to spend her days and nights on the deck because she can't bear to go to her room and walk past all their doors.

One night, a gerbil makes its way to the deck and runs to her for warmth. It's not the smartest animal, but it's figured out that much.

"Now I *have* to go downstairs, don't I?" she says.

She places the gerbil in a pouch in her clothes and drapes a blanket around herself. She finds a closet in the hall downstairs, opens the door, lays the blanket down at her feet, and starts to fill it with things. A cube of pitch, a pitch candle, a wire stand, a metal bowl, a metal spoon, a small wipe cloth, a plank of wood, a hammer, and nails. Then she takes up the corners of the blanket and carries all of it to the room where the gerbils live.

Inside, she takes the gerbil out of the pouch and lowers it gently to the ground. She spots right away where it chewed its way out.

"I will not punish you for this," Naamah says. "You did what you were born to do."

The gerbil's mate comes up and investigates the new smell on the gerbil, the chill the deck left on its fur. The gerbil's mate's teeth are overgrown. One has gotten so long it's curved around the creature's head in a tight spiral, up and around the side, toward the brain.

"You haven't been chewing the way you should, have you? I'll have to come back with the clippers. I don't know why someone hasn't mentioned you. Have you been hiding?"

She sets up the wire stand, arranges the candle beneath it, the metal bowl above, and then places the cube on top. She lights the candle, and while the pitch melts she hammers the plank of wood over the hole that the gerbil made.

"You should let her help you next time."

Once the pitch is melted, she lowers the spoon into it. It immediately starts to firm up at the coolness of the spoon, but she stirs until the spoon is as hot as the pitch. Then she drips the pitch over the new plank of wood.

"I'm going to make this door a little less appealing to chew through. We can't be doing this every night, can we?"

She spreads the pitch with the back of the spoon, a thin, even coat over the entire length of the bottom of the door, starting a little high so she can catch every drip.

"If He regrets you, gerbil, why save you, do you think? When the water recedes, won't you create all the new gerbils just the same? Are you so different, gerbil of the new world?"

The gerbil bites her hard on the leg. She yelps and hits the gerbil smack on the head with the spoon, and it dies instantly. The other gerbil comes over and starts eating him. Naamah smashes her on the head as well.

*I don't know if we brought enough pairs*, she thinks. They were supposed to bring seven pairs of the clean animals, only one pair of the unclean animals, but that seemed too risky to Noah and Naamah. There are at least two pairs of every animal on the boat. But even if she has not driven gerbils to extinction, she wonders, *Am I wicked?*

She lies down and falls asleep there, in the small room, beside the bodies of the gerbils.


WHEN THEY LIVED in the village, a man used to come through every so often, quietly asking for the dead. Once, Naamah came upon him out in the desert, dissecting a body. Around it were bowls, each with a different part of the body she'd never seen.

He flushed at the sight of her. He started apologizing, but she shook her head, insisting she was fine. When he finally relaxed, she asked him to name the parts in the bowls—a liver, a heart. That was the first time she'd seen a full tongue. She didn't realize how far back it went into her throat. In the bowl, it resembled a penis. He commented on her tough stomach. At the time, she'd thought this man's work merely strange; now she wondered if it was wickedness.

Then healers began to come to the village to learn from him. He was not a healer himself, but he taught many men, and many midwives, too. *He cannot be solely wicked*, Naamah thought.

"You have been different since you fell in the water," Shem says.

"Have I?"

"Yes. Worried."

"I think I've been worried this whole time."

Shem smiles. "Something different."

She shrugs.

"Don't pretend you don't know what I mean."

"I'm sorry. You're right."

"What happened when you fell into the water?"

"It hurt. It hurt so much I passed out, and your father rescued me. What about up here? That's where things were really happening."

"Not much."

"You too, huh?"

"Okay, okay. At first, we didn't know you'd fallen in. Dad told us to deal with the wolf, and Japheth took it back to its room. Dad went to the railing, and that's when we realized what had happened. We looked for you in the dark, and you were nowhere. And then the moon came out, and your body came to the surface. The way you rose, back first, in your pale clothes, you looked like a moon yourself.

As soon as Dad saw you, he jumped in. Ham and I grabbed the swing and tied it near where you were and threw it over the side."

"And then?"

"I guess that was when Japheth came back up. He asked us where Dad was, and when we told him you were both in the water, he rushed to the side. But at that point all we could do was wait until Dad had you both back on the swing."

"You pulled me up?"

"Yeah. Dad tried to protect you as he walked up the boat, but you got scraped up pretty bad—you know that. Once you were back on deck, we cleaned and dressed the cuts on your arm and leg."

"Where was Sadie? And Neela and Adata?"

"Trying to quiet the animals. Tossing them feed. They didn't know that you'd fallen." Shem paused. "I was scared."

"I would have been scared if I knew what was happening."

"Don't joke," he says.

"I know." She looks at him. "I love you."

"I love you, Mom."

She hugs him. Over his shoulder, all she can see is water.

## FOUR

When the boat was complete, Naamah gathered the family beside it. On land, the shadow of it was intimidating. They could only guess what it would look like in the water. Naamah prepared them for one last chance for supplies, food, anything they might possibly need. They would not be able to risk leaving the boat again or they, too, could be lost to the rains.

"This is the last time you will see a crowd of people," Naamah said. "Enjoy them. Observe them. Remember what you can. And don't try to stick together. Soon we'll all be together more than we can stand."

Naamah made a gesture for them to head off, and they all did except for Sadie. She walked over to the sunlight right next to the shadow of the boat, closed her eyes, and tilted up her head. Naamah walked over to her.

"We will still have sunlight on the boat."

"I know. But it feels so good."

Naamah closed her eyes, too.

———

NAAMAH WALKS UP TO HAM on the deck. "Neela is beginning to show," she says.

"You noticed?"

"Of course I noticed."

"We're in love."

"I'm not mad," she says. When he shoots her a look, she adds, "I'm not that mad." She waits for him to say something, but he's always been able to wait her out. "And that's not all it is—both so passionately in love."

"We're also bored," he admits.

Naamah laughs. "How is she feeling now?"

"Less bored."

Naamah laughs again. "Does she feel sick at all?"

"No, just tired."

They look out over the water.

"Are you happy for us?"

"Very happy." She wraps her hand around the back of his head and pulls him down to her, kisses his forehead. "Very happy."

"Should we announce it?"

"Yes, that's a very good idea. Let's have a party. Let's celebrate."

"Neela would love that."


WHEN NAAMAH GAVE BIRTH the first time, she was surprised by how large her stomach stayed after he was out. They tried to hand her Japheth, expecting her to reach out, to rest him on her chest. But she was screaming for them to check that another child was not still inside of her, waiting to be born. They gave Japheth to Noah.

They tried to assure Naamah there was not another child. They led her in pushing out the placenta, and they showed it to her. It was floppy in the midwife's hands, but when she got it angled right, it looked like someone had painted a tree on a decaying bag of blood.

She asked for her son. She held him and stroked his cheek and balanced him on her oversize belly, which she trusted to be empty, like the bladders they used as water bags, which she remembered, as a child, blowing up with air.

In a few days, her stomach shrank back into her body. She tried sleeping on her belly for the first time in months, but it felt like she was sleeping on some object that had been misplaced in the bed.

She arranged blankets around her body to rest Japheth on as she nursed him. They made her hot. She spent most of her time naked in the tent, cool cloths draped around the back of her neck, the baby sleeping, naked in a nest of blankets of his own. She'd tried laying him flat, but he wouldn't have it. His shoulders rested above the bed, his legs raised as if he were trying to cradle himself. And his legs were quick to move and startle him out of sleep. His body worked against itself, just as hers did.

Because the nest was the solution for him, she wondered if there was an equally simple, physical solution for herself, for what she was feeling. But if there was, she wasn't sure how to discover it. She didn't know how to express the question to other mothers, if it was a question. She told Noah how impressed she was with her body, and he was glad for her, but she'd meant in the way one is impressed by God, with a measure of fear, a respectful distance. She understood why some women stopped leaving their beds in this time of motherhood.

THE EVENING IS COOL. For the party, they bring up three containers of wine they've been saving. Adata prepares fish they've kept packed in salt. Naamah disappears downstairs to wrap a few honey candies she's saved. Then she lets everyone know that dinner is ready.

Like Naamah, Sadie also brings a gift from what she found among the belongings of her room: a little wax pencil, purple through and through. She'd been afraid to draw with it, to use it up. But now she draws something for Neela, a purple figure, an angel maybe. She kisses Neela on the cheek as she gives her the picture and pencil. Her fingertips are marked by little purple stains.

Everyone but Neela has a cup of wine in hand as they sit around chatting. Neela can't imagine something bitter and dry on her tongue right now.

The boys get out instruments they've been making to perform a song, their present for Neela. Japheth has stretched some leather over a bottomless bucket to make a drum. Ham has found some dried-out gourds that rattle. And Shem has cut a bucket in half and tied some strings across it.

They start to play.

The song is simple but pleasant. Sadie dances around Adata until Adata throws back her head in a laugh, and then she puts her arm around Sadie's waist and spins her, their feet side by side. They step back from each other and switch which direction, which arm is crossing the waist of the other, which hip is touched.

Suddenly Neela squeals, loud as a scream. She's spotted something in the air by Ham's knee as he shakes the gourd. Everyone stops. She points, but she doesn't need to. Fireflies—first one or two, and then suddenly they are everywhere, for the first time since before the rains. Everyone starts hollering and jumping around. Neela cries. She takes them as a sign from God that her child is one He desires to be born.

WHEN NAAMAH HAD ONLY JAPHETH, it was easy to lose track of when she'd bathed him, clipped his nails. But with three little boys, everything was such an ordeal, always a series of actions. Every night they lined up naked, and she would check them, finding scrapes, knees covered in dirt, and once a tick, tucked behind an ear.

Once a week, as Naamah clipped one boy's nails, the other two boys were expected to entertain him. Shem and Japheth always acted out skits, Shem and Ham sang songs, and Japheth and Ham told riddles. Sometimes Ham would get bored and Shem would tell Japheth an endless joke that didn't make sense.

"Japheth, why did the bird go to the market?"

"Why?"

"Because it wanted to get some seeds that he couldn't get in the tree where he lived and he knew there would be someone at the market with that kind of seed so he brought a big bag with him to buy as many seeds as he could fit in the bag so he could take it home with him and always have the seeds that he liked whenever he was hungry and then he pooped out those seeds. He pooped!"

Japheth laughed. He couldn't help himself. "Hey, does that mean new trees ended up growing by his home that had the seeds he liked in them?"

"Oh yeah!"

Japheth laughed again.

When they were all out at the marketplace, Naamah would count their three heads—*one, two, three, one, two, three*—as they walked between the stands of fruit and pottery, losing sight of them and finding them again.

IT'S GETTING LATE, and all the couples are sitting together, catching fireflies and releasing them, whispering into each other's ears. Naamah has been drinking, more than the others. She kisses Noah.

"We should go for a swim," Naamah says.

"I don't think so."

"Why not?"

"Everyone would have to wait around to pull us up."

"So? They'd do that for us. Wouldn't you all do that?"

But no one responds. They don't have much patience left tonight for Naamah's latest ideas about what might make her happy. They don't realize it's harder for her, trying over and over again to dream up ways to *be* happy, and mostly being wrong.

"Then go to bed!" she says, cheery at first. But then, flatly, "Get out of here."

"You should come to bed, too," Noah says.

"No."

"You should—"

"No. I'm fine where I am."

They all start to stand up and brush off their clothes.

"That's not really true," she continues. "I am not fine where I am. I am on a boat in the middle of a flood that was high enough to cover trees. And wasn't there a mountain to the east of us? Did it cover the mountain? I haven't seen anything in months."

"We saw the fireflies tonight," Neela says, trying to be helpful. Ham takes her hand.

"That we did! That we did, Neela. I don't know how, but we did."

"He calls into being things that were not," Japheth says.

"Yes! Yes! Why is it, then, do you think, Japheth, that we should usher all these animals, if he could just do *that*, on the other side of the flood?"

"Naamah," Noah urges, "not now. It's late."

"They did not deserve to die," Japheth says.

Noah hangs his head.

"Then the others animals *did*, you think?" Naamah asks.

"Yes," Japheth answers quickly, but he feels cruel saying it. "In a way."

"That's what I'm getting at now! In what way?"

"Their death was merciful," Japheth says.

"The death itself or the fact that they're now dead?"

Noah tries again. "Naamah, please."

"If *being dead* is merciful," Japheth says, "they had to go through the act of dying to get there—here—you know what I mean."

"Yes, I do. And Japheth—"

Adata interrupts. "Leave him be, Naamah."

Naamah looks at her.

"Nothing he could say would please you."

Naamah can't take her eyes off of Adata. Maybe because she's standing up to her, maybe because of something else.

"Think of the heavens, Naamah," Adata says. "Their starry host was made by the breath of His mouth. The animals are here. You are here. His understanding has no limit, but yours does."

Naamah puts down her cup without looking away and says, "I guess I want to know where the limit to my understanding is. Ask me a question, Adata, that I cannot consider."

On their last day away from the boat, Naamah didn't follow her own advice. Instead of going to the market, she went to see Bethel.

"The sun has darkened you," Bethel said.

"I've been working." Naamah thought she was going to rush into what she wanted to say, but Bethel had a way of slowing everything down.

"You look beautiful," Bethel said.

"Thank you."

"What have you been working on?"

"That's what I came to tell you about. We're about to leave. On an ark. I've been building an ark these last years."

"Just you?"

"No. My entire family."

"Why?"

"God told Noah to."

"That's certainly a reason."

"It's because God is going to send rains—a flood. He wants to wipe the earth clean, start fresh. He's deemed everything wicked and evil. He's seen too much violence. He thinks He got us wrong."

"How does God get something wrong?"

"Right? I . . . I've tried asking that, and they all treat me like I don't make sense. Then I tell you, and it's your first question. It *is* the first question, isn't it?"

"I guess it is."

"I don't want to leave you," Naamah says.

"But God has said you must."

"Yes, but God has already gotten something wrong."

"It's not about whether what He commanded you to do is right or wrong; it's that He commanded it. And I wouldn't see you punished for that." She took Naamah's face in her hands. "I could not see it."

"And what about me seeing *you* punished?"

"Oh, death is not punishment." She released Naamah's face and stepped back. "I am ready to die."

"What if it is a terrible death?"

"If it will make you happy, I will take care of it before the rains."

"You say that as though it's some kind of errand."

"It *is* an errand. I thought it would have come for me already, but if it still hasn't when the rains come, I will go to greet it."

Naamah shook her head.

"Do you still love Noah?"

"I do."

"Then be with him, and your children. Know that I am well."

"Don't you love me more than this? Stow away with us! I will sneak away to see you."

"If it's a matter of how much I love you, then I guess I don't love you enough. But I don't think it's that. God sees fit to enact this death. I see my tiredness on the earth in His tiredness of us."

Naamah began to cry.

"Why have you come to tell me this today?" Bethel asked.

Naamah couldn't answer her.

"Is this the last time I will see you?"

Naamah tried to turn from her.

"It is, isn't it?"

She nodded.

"Pull up your skirt."

Naamah did. Bethel put her middle two fingers in her own mouth, then slid them into Naamah, and pulled her close. Naamah kissed her while Bethel spun her fingers in her, spun them until the tight, circular muscle loosened, and then Bethel slid all her fingers in. Naamah kissed her until she could no longer control her mouth. Bethel pressed on something inside her and Naamah grunted loud enough that anyone nearby could hear. She didn't care that day. She didn't care if everyone knew.

NOAH STEPS in front of Naamah to block her from staring at Adata. "You don't have to ask her any question, Adata. Please go to bed. Everyone, go to bed."

And they did, leaving Noah and Naamah alone on the deck.

"You didn't have to embarrass me," Naamah says.

"I didn't. I mean, you needn't feel embarrassed. No one is giving it another thought."

"Why do you worry about me?" Naamah asks. "Aren't we protected?"

"Naamah, stop trying to goad Him."

"I'm not."

"You are. But He doesn't listen to you."

"Then why worry?"

"Because what if you do provoke Him, Naamah? What if you did accomplish that somehow? Then what?"

"Maybe He deserves it."

"You're doing it again!"

"I'm tired of being on this boat!"

"So am I!" he yells. "We all are. You can see that, can't you?"

"I killed a gerbil the other day."

"What?"

"Two."

"Okay."

She looks at him as if she's just asked him a question.

"What do you want from me?" he says.

"I want you to judge me."

"It's not my place to judge you."

"But you want to?" she asks.

"Not for killing two gerbils."

"But you do want to?"

"Would that be enough for you?"

"Yes."

"Okay, then, yes. I want to judge you for things you have done, things you have said, for nearly dying when the wolf attacked you, for having an overall recklessness toward yourself when you could be safe—*should* be safe. I love you, and I need you to make it through this."

"You thought I should die."

Noah doesn't respond at first.

"You thought—"

"That was a long time ago," he says.

"Not that long."

"It feels like it was. That I could never have felt that way."

"About me."

"I could never have felt that way about you."

"Okay," she says.

"Okay," he says, and he walks off without looking back at her. "I'm going to bed."

She leans her back against one of the beams that holds up the roof.

WHEN NAAMAH IMAGINED the rains beginning, she thought they would appear far across the desert, giving them all time to take cover as the rains made their way across the land. She imagined the whole family would huddle in a room together until they felt like splitting up. That maybe they'd say how grateful they were for each other.

But when the rains actually came, they were busy with tasks all across the boat. Naamah was down in the seed room. She ran as fast as she could to the trapdoor that would block off the deck, but Noah had just closed it. He was soaked with rain, and so were the stairs and the floor beneath him.

She was out of breath.

"Are you okay?" he said.

"Are you?"

He nodded.

"I wanted to see it," she said.

"There's nothing to see."

"But I wanted to see it," she said again.

He climbed back up the stairs. Once he had positioned himself under the door, bracing himself, he waved her up to join him. She climbed up, crouching against his body.

"Ready?" he asked.

"Yes," she said.

He lifted the door and a sheet of water rolled in off the deck. She pushed her head up until she could see over the deck, past the railing. It was just gray. It was not at all like being washed, but rather clouded with dirt.

"Naamah," Noah said, "I have to close it."

She lowered her head again. They were both soaked now.

"I'll clean this up," she said, but that was instinct alone. In fact, she stayed quite still. She thought she might faint. But then the boys started to arrive, coming out of different dark hallways, asking if it had really begun.


DRUNK AND ALONE NOW on the deck, Naamah says aloud, "I was wrong." She yells, "It wasn't enough." And then, speaking more normally again, "I want You to judge me. I don't understand how I could have been judged differently from all those other people. All those children."

She looks out at the sky. She can see stars as they near the horizon of water, can see their dimmer counterparts on the surface. She knows both will disappear as the sun rises—it doesn't matter that one is real and one isn't.

"I'm starting to accept that You will not judge me. Or that You have already passed judgment, and it doesn't have much to do with me. I get it! You determined me *not* wicked, even if I feel otherwise. You are telling me, 'It is not so!' Okay! I'll try to behave accordingly. Which I guess means I will continue to be myself!"

She picks up a cup of wine someone's left, drinks it down, and then finds another. She walks closer to the railing.

"What about you, angel? Have you decided yet? Have you been watching? Has it bothered you that I haven't been down again? Maybe I wanted to see if you would visit me up here—did you think of that?" She leans over the railing and yells, "I guess not!"

It's too dark to see even the water. Those stars at the horizon are the only lights in the sky. Above her, where the moon must be, and the brightest stars, the sky is covered by thick clouds. She would call them gray, but it's too dark for that. Everything is without light. Almost entirely without light, except for the stars at the horizon, as if it's a seam where the sky and water meet, and the thread does not fill the holes that were made for it.

Naamah keeps yelling. "Can I blame something on you, angel? I'll accept anything! I can't keep blaming Him and myself, Him and myself, back and forth. I will blame you for my desire for foods that no longer exist and that I don't know how to make! How about that?" She drinks from the cup. "Every time I think I smell something that isn't animal shit, I think it's a food I almost recognize, and then I imagine that food, and I get a craving so deep that I want to fill it with my own flood!

"I'm blaming that on you from now on, angel! Does that bother you? I would be bothered by that, I think. You know what I'd say, if I were an angel of the Lord? *Don't lay your shit on me*, I think I'd say. But that's just me. What do *you* say, angel?" She waits for what feels like a long time, listening, as if she might actually hear something back.

"For fuck's sake, angel, answer me!" she shouts, and throws the cup overboard. She's expecting a splash, the small pop of a cup dipping under water and then coming back up with its buoyancy, the sound of water receiving things it doesn't intend to drown.

Instead, in the darkness, she hears the cup hit the hard earth.

## FIVE

Naamah begins by dreaming everything a fish. Noah. Each of her sons. Each of their wives. Each of the animals on the boat. Then the boat itself. Ten thousand heart-sized fish.

Then Naamah dreams she's buried in a cloud, a cloud that exerts tremendous pressure all over her body—the dream mismatching one thing with another, as dreams do. Before she thinks to panic, she hears a voice.

"But what is a woman?" it says.

Naamah crawls through the cloud until her head pops out.

A second voice answers, "A woman is a type of human."

"Then why call her a woman instead of a human?"

Naamah twists her body in the cloud, looking for the people talking.

"They have different parts."

"What do you mean?"

"Look closely. They're shaped differently."

"Yeah, but, like, *all* humans are shaped differently. Look over there."

Naamah spots another woman, stuck in a cloud just as she is. Perched near her is a bird, gesturing with his wing to a strangely tall person down on the earth.

"Okay, but their inside parts are different, too," the woman says.

"I mean, my inside parts aren't the same as other cockatoos, but— that's *private*, I think."

The bird is a goliath cockatoo—Naamah remembers seeing one for the first time when fourteen of them suddenly appeared in the desert, feathers black and gray and blue, cheeks red, approaching with their wings spread in a frightening display.

"I don't know what to tell you," the other woman's head says. In her black, plaited hair, bits of gold jewelry keep catching the light.

"Humans can't see inside me, can they?" says the cockatoo.

"No. They can't see inside you."

"Come on—you know. I can tell you know. What is a woman?"

"A woman has something inside her that lets her grow a child," says the woman.

"Is that all that important? I mean, some cockatoos lay eggs and some don't."

"A woman can't lay an egg. She grows the child in her for months. And then she feeds the child with other parts of her body. Other parts that men don't have."

"That sounds horrible," the cockatoo says.

"I am, maybe, not doing the best job explaining."

"Is there anything, outside of the physical, that makes a woman a woman?"

"I guess a woman is someone who doesn't feel like a man."

Finally Naamah interrupts. "Yes!" she yells. "Wait."

The cockatoo and woman are startled. The cockatoo flies over to Naamah and lands on her head.

"Who are you?"

"Get off my head."

"Who are you?" The cockatoo's claws dig into her.

"My name is Naamah. Now get off my head."

The cockatoo perches just above her instead, still uncertain if he should allow her to see him. He sees a little blood in her hair.

"Who are you?" Naamah asks.

"I'm a cockatoo. I don't have a name."

"Do you want a name?"

"What?"

"Do you want a—"

"No, I heard you. People just don't usually go there next. They just call me *cockatoo*, or they never think about it again."

"Well, I can name you. If you want."

The cockatoo takes a few steps one way and then another. "Yes, I want that."

"Okay. I name you Jael."

"Jael?"

"It means *one that ascends*."

"I like that."

"I'm Sarai," the other head yells over.

"How'd you get here?" Naamah asks.

"I'm dreaming," she says.

"No, you're not," says Jael.

"What about you, Naamah?"

"Yes." Naamah tries to recall. "Yes, I got drunk and fell asleep."

"Well, you're not dreaming. I'm not a figment of somebody else's imagination and certainly not of two imaginations at once. That doesn't make any sense."

"It doesn't," Naamah says.

"I wouldn't rule it out," Sarai says.

"I was dreaming things into fish."

"There you go," Jael says. "That was your dream. This is something else."

THEN NAAMAH is falling out of the sky. Then she's standing in the desert. She throws up. When the smell of her own vomit reaches her nose, she thinks, *Maybe it's not a dream.*

In front of her is the man who dissects corpses. In front of him is the dead body of a woman, or the body of a dead woman, or the dead body of a dead woman, or the corpse of a woman, a woman's corpse, a cadaver, her remains. With her split open, with the lappet-faced vultures circling, she is a carcass, carrion.

Her torso is empty, each organ placed neatly in a bowl. He's working on removing her eyes.

"Which is her uterus?"

He looks up from his work and points at a bowl.

She reaches to pick it up, but stops herself. "May I have this?"

He lifts an eye out of the woman's face. The perfect sphere appears wet for a second; then the desert air takes that moisture for itself, striving for an equilibrium it will never reach. Without looking away from his work, he nods.

She picks up the uterus, inspects it. It fits in her hand even with her fingers bent. She wonders what it would be like to fill it, and a pile of rounded pebbles appears by her feet. She sits down on the dusty earth and starts putting pebbles in. She hears each one click against the others. Soon it seems full, but it keeps taking pebbles, and more pebbles keep appearing in the pile.

She sits there for a long time, set on her task. The man leaves, taking a few organs he's interested in dissecting. The vultures come down to eat the body. They are not bothered by Naamah or the soft tapping of the pebbles in the sac of flesh. They eat the skin and meat and then begin to break and eat the bones.

Naamah isn't distracted by the sound. She is focused on the sound of the pebbles sliding over one another, scratching against one another as she works. It's hard to hear anything but the pebbles now, as if she is hearing the sounds of the pieces of the universe arranging and rearranging themselves.

When the vultures leave, the body is in shambles. With enough wind and sand, with a few coyotes, tomorrow it will be hard to tell a body was ever here. But what does that matter? Soon Naamah is sitting atop the uterus, holding and filling it in continual, near-mechanical motion—until it becomes the size of a planet.

She gets up and starts to walk across it.

Jael is in the sky there. "Where did you go?" he asks.

"I just made this planet."

"No, no, no," Jael says, "this is the planet that was below us back when we were talking in the clouds."

Suddenly, she notices other people around her. The strangely tall person appears over her shoulder. Naamah drops to the ground, feels it with her hand to see if the surface of the planet is still the stretched-out flesh of the uterus, but she can't tell. *What would that feel like*, she thinks, *stretched that thin and that full of stone?*

"Where is Sarai?" Naamah asks.

"Up there," Jael says.

Naamah looks up and sees Sarai's head, still suspended in the cloud. But then the world starts to spin, and she does, too, until she spins right into the center of the planet she has created.


THERE, AT THE CENTER, the stones enter Naamah's mouth, and her vagina, and they fill her until she becomes a giant stone woman filled with a giant stone world-baby. She starts to walk through the heavens.

Jael flies around her head. "Are *you* a woman, Naamah?"

"Yes." Naamah is surprised at how difficult it is to move her giant stone lips.

"You look like a dead volcano that grew legs." Jael lands on her head. He sees a ruby there, where the blood had been.

"Dead things can't grow legs," she says.

"Most living things can't grow new legs either," he says.

Jael picks up the ruby and places it in his own eye. Naamah spots the sparkle of it as Jael flies around her.

"Jael," she says, "you have ascended into the heavens."

"Just like my name!"

"Yes, but how? How are you here?" she asks.

"I am dreaming."

Naamah keeps walking, gaining distance on other planets and stars.

"I figured it out," he says. "You and Sarai couldn't both have dreamed me up, so I must have dreamed up both of you. That would be easy."

Naamah doesn't feel cold or warm. Her stone skin no longer registers such sensory things. She tries running her right hand up her left forearm. *No*, she thinks, *nothing*.

"How can you be a woman if you have no body?"

"I have a body," Naamah says.

"You have a shape—I'll give you that."

Naamah looks down at herself and thinks he may be right. "I still feel like a woman," she says.

"Let me go in," he says. "I'll figure it out."

She opens her mouth and Jael flies in. She wants to swallow him immediately, but he perches on a rise along the edge of a molar.

"Don't bite down on me now," he says.

If she responds, she'll crush him, break all his hollow bird bones.

"Maybe you are a woman in your heart," Jael says. "I'm going to see." He flies down her throat and squeezes through the stone wall near her heart. He travels from the vena cava into the right atrium of the heart.

"Pump your heart, Naamah."

Naamah is surprised—her heart has been still this whole time—

but he's right: she can control it with a thought. She triggers a heart-beat, and Jael flies into the right ventricle faster than he expected, shrouding his head in his wings for protection. Then he's pushed out to the lungs. He rests there, tucks himself into an alveolus, doesn't let the heart pull him back yet. He likes the little cave of the little berry within her.

Naamah can't feel him there. She's focused on keeping her heart beating. She's so focused she's stopped walking, and her motionless body projects the sound of her beating heart louder than anything else in the universe.

Jael lets his body be carried back to the heart, into the left atrium and then the left ventricle, then out of the heart through the aorta. As he tumbles through, he spreads his wings and stops himself. Naamah can't see him, but if she could, she'd tell him he looks like an angel in a holy hall.

Then Jael gathers himself and flies straight upward, through layers of stone that seem to part just enough for his body to push through. Soon he's out of her neck, landing on her shoulder, which is like a large, flat peninsula projecting out into space.

"You can stop beating now," he says.

She relaxes.

"You were not a woman in your heart."

"I wasn't?"

"Not distinctly."

"I'm going to keep walking," she says.

"Where are you going?"

"Away. Farther."

"I think you should be going *to* somewhere."

"I think you should have exploded by now." That sounded rude. She adds, "Without the pressure of the atmosphere around you."

"I have the force of you around me, Naamah."

The fish come back and eat her, stone by stone. It takes a long time.

"Please, stop," Naamah says.

When Naamah finally returns to her normal form, the fish are dead under her feet, bodies piled high, their bellies swollen with stones. She slides down them until her feet touch the ground. She rubs her toes in the dirt until her feet feel dry and smooth.

Jael is still with her, and she's not sure what she's done to deserve him. In some light he appears blue, but she likes it best when the light turns his feathers perfectly black. He's the first animal she's enjoyed looking at in months.

As Naamah walks away with Jael on her shoulder, a family of striped hyenas passes them, to feast on the fish. She worries that she'll return later to find hyenas with too many stones in their bellies, dead near the fish they could not eat, and near them dead vultures, dead hooded crows. One dead animal leading to another.

Naamah and Jael see a throne in the distance. As they approach it, they make out Sarai sitting on the throne.

"It's so good to see you again," she says. She sounds different from before. More confident maybe, now that she's in her rightful place.

"You too," says Naamah.

"What are you doing here?" asks Jael.

"I am queen of all things."

Jael looks around. "What things?"

"All things," she says again. "I've decided."

"Like a god?" Naamah asks.

"Yes," Sarai says.

"Isn't that blasphemous?" Naamah says.

"Heresy!" says Jael. "Profanity. Sacrilege." Sounding more like a cockatoo than ever before. "Impiety. Desecration. Irreverence."

"Stop!" Sarai says. "It is not any of those things because it is the truth."

"Are you saying you are God?" Naamah says.

"*Like* a god. For now."

"You were more interesting to talk to before," says Jael.

Sarai laughs. "Have you figured out what a woman is, Jael?"

"No." He shakes his cockatoo head. "Have you?"

"Mmm. I've been considering it."

A female lion approaches them, pulling an ibex by its torn neck, letting one of the ibex's horns drag along the ground, making a sharp line in the dirt before the body smears through it.

"I find I am less quick to violence than the men I have known, though I'm as capable of it," Sarai says.

The lion stops and drops the ibex beside the throne and looks to Sarai, who nods at her. Then she starts to eat.

"What violence have you committed?" Jael asks.

"I have cut off a man's penis who forced it into my mouth."

Jael whistles. The sound of the lion eating is loud and wet, and sometimes something squeaks. Naamah feels queasy.

"Truthfully, I would have bitten it off if it wouldn't have filled my mouth with blood."

A vision of Sarai flashes before Naamah's eyes: Sarai, covered in blood and grinning.

"When was this?" Naamah asks.

—————

TIME REWINDS. The lion takes the ibex away. Jael and Naamah move back from the throne.

This time, when they walk through the desert, they come upon an Egyptian vulture.

"Who are you?" asks Jael.

"I am the voice of the Lord," says the vulture.

"Get the fuck out," says Jael.

"Wouldn't that make you an angel?" Naamah asks.

"Yes," says the vulture.

"You should name him," Jael says into Naamah's ear.

"I am the Metatron."

"That's not a name," says Jael.

"You might know me as Enoch."

"Noah's great-grandfather?" Naamah asks.

The vulture nods its head. "But I am not Enoch now."

"Do you know who I am?" she says.

"Yeah, do you know who we are?" Jael says.

"You are the wife of Noah. And you are a cockatoo."

"No! I am Jael!" he yells. "And this is Naamah."

The vulture spots a hyrax nearby. The hyrax freezes and begins to bark. The vulture freezes, too.

"Are you hungry?" Naamah asks, surprised.

The vulture doesn't respond.

"Vulture!" Jael says.

The vulture looks back to them, but then back to the hyrax.

Time rewinds again.

THIS TIME, when they walk through the desert, the earth is slowly becoming the deck of a boat. Naamah begins to panic.

"I am waking up," she whispers to Jael.

"No, you are in my dream, remember?"

"Jael, come find me, will you?"

"When I wake up, I won't be able to speak."

"Jael—" Naamah stops.

"What? What is it?"

She turns to him. "Are you on the boat, Jael?"

"What boat?"

"When you fell asleep, where were you?"

"It was dark. It's easy to fall asleep there."

Naamah's panic is rising. Her chest begins to hurt. "No," she says to herself. "No, no."

"It doesn't matter, Naamah. You are not real. I dreamed you, Naamah. Relax. Relax."

She crouches and puts her head between her knees, the dirt still turning to wood beneath her. Her ears are pounding. Her chest feels stiff, as if it, too, were made of wood.

WHEN SHE CAN STAND AGAIN, Jael is gone. The dream boat looks like the real boat. The only reason she knows she is not awake is that now she's the one who's made of fish. The fish of her body come out orange and shining. The fish of her vagina come out red. All the fish of her swim into the sky, and together they bring on the dawn.

# SIX

Adata comes back up the stairs. "Are you alone?" she asks, and Naamah wakes up, still sitting with her back against a beam of the railing.

"Of course I'm alone. You are alone, too."

"You're still drunk," Adata says, and she sits beside her.

"I am. And I just discovered we are on land."

"What are you talking about?"

"I don't know how I didn't realize it earlier. The ship has felt strange under my feet for a while now—still rumbling, but like an echo of how it was when we were moving."

"How do you know we're not moving now?"

"I threw my cup over and it hit the ground," Naamah says. "I heard it."

"Naamah—"

"Yes! I heard it!"

"What does that mean for us?"

"Nothing. There's still only water. You can hear how the wind passes over it. Who knew that sounded so different from wind passing over land, but it does."

Adata stops to listen.

"What are you doing back up here?" Naamah asks.

Adata takes a deep breath, unsure of how to start. "I saw how you were looking at me earlier."

"How was I looking at you earlier?"

"Like you wanted to eat me," Adata says.

"No. I would never hurt you."

"I'm not saying you would."

Naamah's too drunk to follow, so Adata slides her hand onto Naamah's thigh. Naamah looks at her hand and then at Adata and then at her hand again. She sobers up quickly.

"You are the wife of my son."

"I am. Because God said it should be so."

Naamah opens her mouth, but then closes it again.

"Japheth and I are not in love. Ham and Neela are. Shem and Sadie. It's wonderful. But Japheth and I are not. And we understand our situation. I accept my position gratefully. I'm happy to be alive and with you all. I will be a great wife and a great mother." As she says these things, she's arguing for what they might do next.

"And Japheth?" Naamah asks.

"Japheth will find happiness again." Adata's making a promise like it's a trade.

"You are sure?"

"I will make sure of it." She continues to move her hand higher on

Naamah's thigh. "I want to be happy, Naamah." She's in her ear now. Her pointer finger has reached her vulva but lingers just outside.

"Aren't you too young?" Naamah says, but only because she thinks she should. At this point, Adata can have anything she wants.

"I am old enough." Adata reaches the rest of her fingers around the flesh of Naamah's ass, grips her while her pointer finger stays on Naamah's edge.

But Naamah blurts out, "I left a lover in the flood." She feels like she might die, having finally said this out loud.

Adata says, "So did I."

Naamah raises herself up and swings her leg around so that she's straddling Adata. She kisses her. She kisses her down her neck, and they both slide their bodies down until they are lying on the deck. She pulls down the loose collar of Adata's dress and takes her breast in her mouth, flicks her nipple with her tongue until it peaks, then sucks on it, swipes her full tongue around it. She pulls her dress back to cover Adata's nipple, so it doesn't chap in the night air, then goes to her other nipple.

When her chest is covered again, when Naamah has had her fill of her breasts, she raises her clothing until her full stomach is out. Naamah runs her bent fingers, the flats of her nails, against the inside of her thighs. She licks her from the bottom of her vulva to the top of her clitoris, where she sucks on her. Three times she does this. Then she raises her own clothing, lifts one of Adata's legs and places it on her shoulder, then lines up their clits. Adata moves how she wants to from there. Her eyes are closed. Naamah knows she is imagining her lover. She watches Adata's skin and fat and breasts move at the motion of their bodies and thinks of how Bethel's husband watched Bethel.

Adata's orgasm isn't like Bethel's at all. Once she starts shaking with it, she pulls Naamah on top of her and continues to move her hips gently into Naamah's thigh. And then it's over and she raises a shoulder so Naamah knows to get up.

"Will you want to do that again?" Naamah asks.

"I don't know," Adata says.

And Naamah is grateful she is an honest woman.

In the morning, the family tries to understand why the boat has stopped. The boys and their wives run back and forth, looking over one railing and another, calling out what they see. But all anyone can see is water. More and more water. Except for the small patch of earth where Naamah's cup fell.

They collect all the ladders on the boat and fashion a ladder long enough to reach the earth. Each person climbs down and wades toward the little bit of land. They begin to understand it more, this odd, shallow place the boat has struck, rocky and hidden.

When they reach the land, they jump up and down, testing it under their feet. Eventually Shem laughs. Ham splashes him, and then they all start splashing each other. Naamah falls backward, into the water, laughing hard.

But soon there's nothing else to do, and they return to the boat.

Below deck, a ewe is about to lamb. Naamah is excited; maybe she won't have to feed the lambs to a lion or a leopard. She would be happy if the lambs could stand on the earth for even a minute before she had to take them back to another animal's mouth. She thinks of the bears on the boat, appreciates how well they can survive on seeds and nuts.

But then she looks back down at the patch of land, thinking, *If the water is receding, will I lose my chance to see the angel again?*

WHEN JAPHETH WAS YOUNG, he was so bullheaded that they wondered if he could hear at all. Naamah would spot him heading toward a big stick, certain that he was going to pick it up and swing it near his little brothers' heads. "Japheth!" she would cry out. But soon enough the stick was in the air and the little ones were laughing, running off to find sticks of their own. When she yelled at Shem and Ham, they stopped immediately. It wasn't until Naamah caught Japheth's eye and stared him down that he'd drop his stick.

So one day, when there was not even the slightest wind, Naamah decided to test Japheth's hearing. She took him out to a place in the desert where there was not a bird, not a snake, nothing. She brought a bag filled with a flute, a lyre, a small drum, little metal pieces she could clang together, little sticks, anything that would produce an especially low or high sound.

"Japheth," she said, "if you tell me honestly every time you can hear a sound—if you don't ignore me, not once—I will get you a whole bag of marbles."

"Really?" he asked.

She nodded.

"Okay," he said.

She sat him down in the dirt. "Now you stay here, and I'm going over here behind you. When I start making sounds, raise your hand if you can hear me," she said as she walked away. "Raise it straight up."

When she was some distance away from him, she whispered, "Can you hear me?"

He didn't move.

She started with the flute and blew the highest note it could make. Japheth raised his hand. She went down the notes, and every time, his hand flew up. She plucked the lyre, banged the sticks, struck the metal, hit the drum.

He heard it all.

She walked back to him with her collection of instruments. She crouched down, putting her face very near to his. "You can hear everything I say, can't you?"

"Not when I'm not paying attention to you," he said.

She nodded, stood up, and started to walk home, almost laughing.

"Are we leaving?" he asked.

She didn't answer him. She couldn't even look at him.

"Do I get a bag of marbles?"

"Yes," she yelled over her shoulder.

She listened to the slap of his sandals behind her. She tried to listen so closely that she could hear his breath.


NAAMAH ASKS JAPHETH to wait on the deck near the ladder, to lower it when she returns.

"Can't we just leave it out?" he says.

"What if the boat shifts and the ladder floats away?"

"The ark isn't exactly the kind of ship that shifts."

"Do it for your mother," she says.

"Fine," he says. He goes to his room and grabs a piece of wood to work on while he waits. He's been carving it into a fox with a small, sharp knife. When he comes back, he finds only a pile of her clothes; she's already in the water. He lifts the ladder back up to the deck.

Naamah starts by swimming with her head above water, long sidestrokes, as if nothing's changed. Something touches her leg, and for a second she's sure it's the angel's hand. But it's a plant that's learned to grow in the constant water. She's too close to the ground here. She'll have to swim farther from the boat, farther from the rising land, before she dives.

On her first dive, she can't bring herself to open her eyes. On her second dive, she opens them and the angel is right in front of her face. She screams and the film appears over her mouth again so that she really does scream into the water.

"I've been waiting for you," the angel says.

"I see that," says Naamah.

"You slept with your son's wife."

"I thought that might've been a dream."

"It wasn't."

"Well, what do you want me to say?"

The angel stops to think. Then she says, "I don't know."

"Show me something," Naamah says.

"Like what?"

Naamah shrugs.

The angel takes off, and Naamah follows. The sea has a tunneling effect, so Naamah tries not to look around, keeps the angel in the center of her focus.

When they come to the climbing side of another mountain, they start to follow around the base of it. The water gets brighter, but it's empty of life. And then she sees a manatee, swimming slowly, its large body fitting snugly between the surface of the water and the earth.

"How? What does it eat?"

"Algae, mostly. It would be much larger if there were more food."

"Is it alone?"

"As far as I can tell."

The manatee has noticed them and comes over.

"Is it safe?" Naamah asks.

"Yes."

Naamah strokes the animal's side as she swims by, and again as she swims back. Then the manatee swims under her and bumps her feet with her soft back. Naamah laughs as she's thrown off balance, the sense of balance she can have in the water.

But then the manatee seems bored with them and swims off.

"Is there anything else alive down here?"

"It is mostly barren."

"Do you know what it will be like when the water's gone?"

"No. But I have been making something. A place for myself. To live."

"Like a house?"

"Yes."

"Will it be ruined if the waters leave?"

"I think it is deep enough."

"Will you show me?"

The angel swims off again. This time she takes Naamah's hand. It's the first time they've touched. Naamah expected something otherworldly, but it feels like a human hand. If this is not the angel's true form, she has done an impeccable job capturing it.

JAPHETH GETS TIRED of waiting and whittling. His little fox is as done as it can be without a little sand and paint, a few little whiskers pressed into the wood.

He goes to find Shem and Ham, to ask them to wait for Naamah on the deck. He knows Shem will say yes. Shem is happy everywhere, and he goes through his life somehow knowing this—that he will be happy wherever he ends up. But not Ham. Ham will need to be persuaded.

So Japheth presents them with a wooden board covered with smooth indentations, along with a bag of marbles, so that they might play a game while they wait.

"It'll be fun," Shem says.

And Ham gives in.

AFTER SWIMMING FOR a long time, Naamah and the angel come to a structure that looks like it's made of water, as if the arch of the doorway appearing before them is a trick of the eye.

"This is bigger than a house," Naamah says.

"Yes."

Naamah sees people inside, walking alone and in pairs. She squeezes the angel's hand.

"They are dead," the angel says.

"That doesn't make me feel better."

The angel pulls her on. "Some were not able to move on, were trapped in the water. I built this for them and decided I would stay."

"If you're an angel, can't you take them to where they were supposed to go?"

"Only if I want to be found as well."

"Do they resent you for that?"

"They don't know what other worlds there are. They can't tell whether one would be better than another. They live here now. That is enough."

"I guess."

"Do you like where you live?"

"The boat? No."

"But you remain there."

"It seems like the only option, doesn't it?"

"So it is for these people, too."

"But they know you."

"You know me, too. You haven't asked me to take you from the boat."

"Is that an option?"

"Technically. But changing your position for the coming years—no, I would draw too much attention to myself."

"So you are a selfish angel?"

"Have you known another kind?"

A dead person approaches them, nods a hello to the angel, and continues on.

"Can they see me?"

"Of course."

"Do they know I am alive? That I'm different from them?"

"I don't know. But it seems obvious to me."

"Yes, yes, you're right."

"Oh."

"What?" Naamah says.

"You were asking about their consciousness."

"Yes," Naamah says. "That's a nice way of putting it."

Naamah cranes her neck to look at the structure now, to take it all in, the dozens of arches, dozens of spires. It looks like a palace, and Naamah's in awe of it.

"Where did you get the inspiration for this place?"

"The heavens."

"Right. Of course you did."

"You don't believe me?"

"No, I do."

"Then why say it like that?"

"Because you're impossible. This is impossible. I've probably banged my head on something in the water and I'm dying alone somewhere."

"No," she says. "You're fine, Naamah."

"And why do *you* say it like that?"

"Because you are fine, but you might also be despicable."

Naamah's face gets hot with a shame that she's not sure she deserves to feel.

SHEM PICKS UP a handful of marbles from a divot in the board and starts placing them in other divots. "Congratulations again, Ham."

"Thanks."

"I was surprised to hear the news. You know, since Mom had said not to have sex on the boat."

"We didn't at first." Ham takes up a handful of marbles now. "Why? Have you and Sadie not had sex?"

"Not yet. It's not so hard not to."

"It's not that I couldn't control myself."

"I wasn't saying that."

"No, I just don't want you to think that's why."

"Then why?"

"Neela felt like we were living as if the waters would never go down. And she had to believe they were going to go down, that we would get off the ark."

"But God said we would survive the flood," says Shem.

"Knowing that to be true and *acting* as if it's true are two different things."

"That's what Neela says?"

"Yeah," says Ham.

"Sounds like Mom."

"No." Ham hadn't thought of that. "No. She's not like Mom."

Shem laughs.

———

A GROUP OF CHILDREN has come up behind Naamah. One asks, "Why is she despicable?"

Another says, "I think she's beautiful."

"Can I braid your hair?"

"Okay," Naamah says.

She feels the hands of many dead children run through her hair, but one takes the lead, gathering a thick plait of her hair on the left, parting it from the rest, running a dead-girl fingernail along her scalp to make the line neat, and then doing it again on the right, making three neat sections. Then she begins to braid.

The first child watches the dead girl's steady work, and asks again, "Why is she despicable?"

Before the angel can respond, Naamah speaks. "Because I question God's will."

"God made the flood, didn't He?" the child asks.

"He did."

The child leans over and whispers in Naamah's ear, "Then I am despicable, too."

Naamah feels tears coming on, stinging, salty enough to turn all the floodwaters into a sea. She tries to focus on the small tugging of her hair.

The angel says, "You could never be despicable, child."

"Of course not," Naamah says.

The child looks unconvinced.

"It's the way I act," Naamah says, "motivated by my question."

"What do you do?" another child says.

"I have hurt people."

"Did you defeat them?" one asks.

"No. Not that kind of hurt."

"Lions hurt other animals," a child says.

"That's true."

"I would be okay if there were no more lions."

"Would you?" Naamah asks.

"Yes."

"If lions didn't hunt the animals who grazed, didn't move them around the fields, then the fields would not yield. Many more animals would die," Naamah explains.

"That's sad."

Naamah nods.

"We don't need to eat anymore," the girl says, the girl who has been braiding Naamah's hair. She peeks out from around her back. "Your braid is finished."

"Thank you," Naamah says. She runs her hand along it.

SOMETIMES BETHEL WOULD come over to Naamah's home and they would bake. Once Bethel wanted to make an orange cake. She'd brought fresh oranges with her, straight from the market. She'd been so excited to see them. She kept holding them up to her nose.

Naamah set to work combining the ingredients. Soon she realized that the cake would take the last bit of oil in the house, the scraped inside of the last vanilla bean, the last eggs, the last flour. It felt like a small miracle to have all the right remaining amounts of all of the ingredients, but not one of God's miracles. One that was born of her own past actions.

"WILL YOU BRAID my hair now?" the dead girl asks.

"Okay," Naamah says.

The girl moves around and stands in front of Naamah, who runs her fingers through her dead-girl hair. It feels a little like water and yet still like hair, as if water were running over the hair constantly without wetting it. It feels like how she thought the angel would feel—Naamah's own estimation of holiness.

When Naamah has finished the braid, she has nothing to tie it with. The angel reaches down and from the water creates a string of crystals around the end of the braid.

"Thank you!" the girl says, and all the children run off laughing.

Naamah turns to the angel. "Is that how you made all of this?"

"Yes."

"Can you show me again?"

The angel thinks for a second, then constructs a small bird of crystal and places it in Naamah's hands. The bird looked sturdy in the angel's hands, but Naamah can hardly feel it. She balances it in one hand and pinches the bird's tail with the other. The crystal of the tail collapses and lengthens into a thinner crystal.

But for a second, Naamah thinks that she's made the tail longer with another crystal, that she has the same power the angel has, to create. And while that second was exhilarating, Naamah feels great relief at not having that power, at having only the ability to deform the crystal.

Now, knowing her small value in this place, her near worthlessness, Naamah is newly excited to explore it, to run her hand along every crystal wall and doorway. But then she stops.

"Is Bethel here?" she asks.

"No," the angel says.

HAM ASKS SHEM, "Does that mean you've never had sex?"

"I have," says Shem. He looks embarrassed.

"But not with Sadie?"

"No. It was when I was younger."

"I've only had sex with Neela."

"Do you think she cares about that?"

"I don't know," Ham says. "Are you worried about what sex will be like with Sadie?"

"No."

"Like if you can't please her?"

"I mean, I already make her orgasm."

"Right, but if you can't please her during sex. From the sex itself."

"Then I guess I'll make her afterward. Or we'll figure it out. Does Neela orgasm?"

"I don't know. How do you know?"

"I think you'd feel it. Sadie shakes, and she kicks her feet after."

Ham considers this.

"But really you should just ask her," says Shem.

"I don't know. We're doing okay."

"I guess so." And Shem laughs again. He's referencing the pregnancy, trying to make a joke, to stop Ham from being so serious. But he's not sure that's how it came out.

NAAMAH ASKS THE ANGEL, "How do you know? Did you know Bethel?"

"I have been watching you since God has been watching you."

"Watching me or Noah?"

"Noah."

"So she definitely isn't here?"

"No."

When Naamah doesn't respond, the angel continues, "It's mostly children here. Most adults knew what to do, how to die."

"What will happen to them?"

"I don't know. As long as they're down here, I will remain with them."

"I should get back to the boat."

"Yes," the angel agrees.

ONCE NAAMAH REACHES THE SURFACE, she yells for Japheth.

Shem walks to the railing while Ham gets the ladder. "It's us, Mom," Shem shouts.

They lower the ladder, but they don't watch her climb it. They don't see the sun catching on the water still on her body, the day turning her more radiant and less human at once. But the angel sees this.

# SEVEN

Noah runs up onto the deck. "The ewe is lambing, Naamah. I thought you might want to come."

"Yes," she says. "I'll follow you."

They go to a large room where they keep all the sheep together. The sheep, in their small herd, are less anxious than some of the other animals. Naamah spots right away that one of the ewes has a lamb's front hooves sticking out of its vagina. The ewe panics as Naamah approaches, but once Naamah gets her hands on her, she pushes her down, places a knee on her, and the ewe is calm.

Naamah holds the lamb's hooves tightly with her left hand. Then she slides her right hand underneath the sheep's tail, under a flap of skin, pale pink, a near half-moon. She moves her hand under the flesh, to the right and to the left and to the right again, until the head of the lamb begins to come forward. Then she grabs it, her hand around the back of the neck, under the ears.

"Now push," she says to the ewe. And she pulls the lamb from the body of the sheep. From the neck, she runs her right hand over the lamb's face and clears the nose of mucus. "Come on," she says, and she pats the lamb on its side. It starts to breathe and sneezes.

Naamah looks up at Noah, who is smiling. He's been standing in the doorway with the door open, to let the air circulate. Behind him is Neela. She looks like she might be sick. Naamah motions to Noah to take her away.

Naamah can see another lamb is coming, so she moves the first lamb to a fresh spot of hay. She then goes through the same actions until the second lamb is out and breathing. She moves the second lamb to be with the first, away from the blood and afterbirth. They are starting to fluff up. They are soft and sweet.

She turns back to the mother, who is already getting back on her feet. "Good job, mama," she says. It's then that Naamah notices that Noah, in tending to Neela, has left the door ajar and some sheep have begun to wander into the halls of the boat.

IN THE DESERT, even on cooler nights, Naamah and Noah would sleep naked next to each other. She liked to lay her hand on his chest. His hair was soft, and the skin underneath was even softer. His hands grew rough. Sometimes his lower arms. Always his cheeks, sun-worn. And if she ever had a day where she'd been bothered by little things he did or failed to do—not helping enough with the boys, not asking her how she felt—somehow her feelings were always eased by ending the day next to the soft skin of his chest. The next day he could do just one lovely thing, tell one perfect joke, and she would remember how difficult it was just to get through life at all. She loved him enormously, and she knew she always would.

"Boys!" Naamah calls out as she leaves the room, closing the door behind her, scanning the hallway for sheep. Neela has found a bucket nearby, and Noah is still with her, standing behind her.

"What happened?" he says.

"The sheep got out."

"Shit. I'm sorry."

"At least they're all right," she says. "Are you going to be okay, Neela?"

Neela nods, stretching one arm behind her and waving them off awkwardly.

"We'll check on you," Naamah says as they hurry away.

Soon Japheth, Ham, Shem, Sadie, and Adata are all there with them. "There should be fourteen full-grown sheep in the room, along with two new lambs, but four sheep have just wandered away," Naamah tells them. "I'm not sure how far they got. Let's split up and get them back."

"New lambs! That's so great, Mom," says Shem.

"I can't wait to see them!" Sadie's beaming like she's the mother.

"After all the sheep are back," Naamah says, "we can play with the babies for a bit. They'll probably be walking around by then."

"See you back here," Japheth says, and he heads off. They split up to cover the decks, with Naamah staying on this one. It looks empty, but there are rooms at the ends that aren't always securely closed, like their bedrooms. She almost expects to find a sheep in her room, chewing on a blanket. But she makes it all the way to the other end of the boat, and all the rooms are empty that should be.

She turns to walk back down the hallway, dark as night in the middle of the boat, and then she hears something. It sounds like one of the cockatoos, repeating one word over and over: "Jael. Jael." She stops to listen, and the word sounds familiar to her, but she can't remember why. She runs her hand along the wooden door. But then she starts walking again, eager to see the sheep.

Noah, Japheth, and Adata are there, standing patiently in a little arc, and they're smiling, looking down at an empty floor.

"What happened? Where did they all go?" Naamah asks.

"We're back up to thirteen sheep, Naamah. We're just admiring the little ones," Noah says.

And then she understands—the way they're standing, their smiles. She feels something bump into her legs, and she instinctively reaches down and shoves away the rough wool of one of the sheep she cannot see. *Just when I actually wanted to see them*, she thinks. Her chest begins to hurt.

"I rushed to the deck, just in case, but no sheep there," Noah says. "Ham is with Neela. Japheth and Adata went one deck down and returned with three sheep. Shem and Sadie went to the lowest deck, and they're not back yet."

Naamah stumbles out of the room, trying to catch her breath. Noah follows her.

"Are you okay?"

She feels dizzy. "I need to swim," she says. *The angel can fix this.*

"Right now?" Noah asks.

"Yes. But I'll just be a minute. I'll leave the ladder down. I promise." And she leaves him, his body still leaning toward her in the darkness of the hallway.

BELOW THEM ALL, Sadie and Shem search the lower deck together. This level is darker and colder than the rest. Usually Sadie wraps herself in a blanket before walking around down here, but they came so fast.

It's not hard to hear where the sheep has headed as they start down the hallway. It's somewhere down at the end, confused and lonesome, maybe having stumbled into a small room.

But just as Naamah had unsettled the walrus, the sheep's sad bleating has awoken some of the larger animals.

NAAMAH WADES OUT from the patch of land and gets under the water. She swims to where it gets deep, and the angel is there.

"Give it back," Naamah says.

"Excuse me?" The angel's voice is calm, almost polite.

"My ability. To see the animals. Give it back to me."

"I don't know what you mean."

"When I was on the boat, I had stopped being able to see the animals. Then I met you and I could see them again. And now it's gone again. I just helped these two beautiful lambs into this world and I can't see them anymore. You must have taken it from me. You must have taken it back."

"Naamah, I didn't do anything to you."

"Yes, you must have—and you can undo it. I need to see them again."

"I'm sure you can regain it, if you have before. But it has nothing to do with me."

"No—"

"You're quick to assign blame where there is none."

"No!"

"Naamah." The angel's face drops. "You must get back to the ark."

"You can—"

"Naamah," she says again, "get back."

Naamah realizes something is wrong. The angel pulls her hands back along the sides of her rib cage, pushes forward with her palms, and Naamah flies backward through the water. She spins herself around and swims as fast as she can, to the land, the ladder, the boat.

SHEM AND SADIE hear the scratching of claws, but they continue down the hall. They reach the sheep and usher it back toward the stairs, Sadie in front and Shem behind. As they approach the scratching again, they hear a growl. It scares Sadie.

"We can go faster, if you want," Shem says.

That's when they hear the first pound—the sound of an animal launching itself into its door. The wood begins to splinter.

"Run, Sadie!" Shem is right beside the door when the second pound comes, and with it, the door breaks. Shem is one step ahead of the door as the animal crashes into the other side of the hallway, driven by its own force: a polar bear.

As it scrambles for its footing, the bear swings a paw at Shem, catching his leg.

NAAMAH CLIMBS THE LADDER, grabs her clothes but doesn't bother dressing.

"Noah!" she screams. "Noah!"

They run into each other on the stairs.

"Is everyone okay?" she asks.

"Shem and Sadie still aren't back."

"We need to find them."

They run together down the stairs.

SHEM YELLS OUT in pain as he runs. The sheep is frozen in the hallway and he climbs over it. The bear lashes out at the sheep next, and the moment's distraction gives Shem and Sadie time to make it up the stairs. At the top there is a stronger door, a barricade, for emergencies like this.

This is where Naamah and Noah find them. Through the door, they can hear the bear filling itself with the warmth of the sheep. Shem passes out from the pain, and Sadie screams. Noah scoops him up.

"He will be okay, Sadie," Naamah says. She follows Noah to the deck. They bring out water, soap, a needle and thread, and cloth to wrap the wound. They wash his leg, and Shem wakes again. Noah gives him a bit of cloth to bite down on. Sadie is waiting nearby, knowing not to get close.

Three of the five cuts are deep enough that they need stitches. It's hard for Shem not to pull his leg away, so Noah sits on his chest, facing away from him, holding his leg down with both hands above the knee. As Naamah stitches the biggest cuts shut, the skin is pulled. She's worried about the remaining two cuts opening further, so they each get a stitch, too.

Noah nods that she's done well, and he gets off of Shem's chest. He dries and wraps Shem's leg, and Sadie rushes over and kisses Shem hard on the mouth.


JAPHETH AND ADATA ARE DOWNSTAIRS, waiting at the barricade to see what the bear will do next. When it's quiet, they go in. The hall is covered in blood, but the bear and dead sheep are gone. The bear dragged it back to its room, its odd den. Japheth and Adata set to work fixing the door while the bear is still eating. After this little feast, if the bear conserves its energy, it might not need to eat again for a month. And they are hoping that the water will be gone by then.

They get long planks of wood from a closet to reinforce the door. Then they start to clean the blood. Neither of them feels sick or queasy, and they're glad to know they have each other for the times ahead.


NOAH HELPS SHEM TO BED, but Naamah tells Sadie to follow her. They walk back toward the room with the sheep. They pass Neela and Ham, and tell them what's happened. Ham goes off to be with Shem, and Naamah pulls Neela along with her and Sadie.

When they get to the room, Naamah encourages them to play with the lambs, whose knees still buckle. So the women sit down and pretend to forget everything that has happened that day, and they play. And though Naamah cannot see the lambs, she enjoys watching two of her daughters-in-law laughing and happy.

SOON AFTER THE RAINS STOPPED, Naamah had brought buckets of dirt from the storage room up to the deck and filled a very large, low frame with it all. She gathered manure from the cows and horses and mixed it in with the dirt. Then she went down to her seeds. She took a cup of grass seed, and then cups of clover and forb seeds, too, and brought them back to the deck in a cloth bag. She half-filled a bucket with water, placed the bag inside, and put on a lid. For days she tended the dirt in the frame and swapped out the water in the bucket. Soon the seeds were sprouting.

She poked holes into the dirt with her finger, row after row, then dropped a seed into each hole. She pinched the holes closed and the dirt fell to cover the seedlings. Soon a little pasture was growing on the deck. Naamah wanted to lie in it but didn't trust that it wasn't a fragile thing.

She was thrilled that soon she would be able to pick grass from it and offer it to a cow or sheep. She was thrilled that soon, after she'd taken her hand to its rich surplus and removed as much as she could, complete with sounds of tearing and ripping, no one would be able to tell. Her actions would be undetectable. Her presence would mean little.

———

THE DAY AFTER THE LAMBS are born, early in the morning, the family takes the lambs out on the land, in the sun, to help them dry out. Naamah watches from the deck, worried she'll knock a lamb into the water in her blindness. Noah stays behind to keep her company.

From above, Naamah watches her sons and daughters-in-law, figuring where the lambs are by the way her family moves. She can hear the lambs' young hooves even through her family's excited cooing. The bandage on Shem's leg shows that some blood has made it through during the night.

"We'll change it when he gets back to the deck," Noah says, watching her eyes, knowing what she's thinking.

ABOUT A MONTH after the rains stopped, Naamah heard a great rustling in one of the rooms near her own. Nothing bad had happened with any of the animals yet—no one hurt, no door broken, everything according to plan—and she was feeling bold. She entered the room.

The walls and floor of the room were covered with atlas moths, a thousand of them, some clustered in corners, others flying clumsily through the air. Naamah stepped inside and shut the door behind her. She thought she should be scared, but instead it comforted her, how this room no longer looked like a room, the walls and floor shifting in shapes of red and brown. The ends of the moths' wings looked like the heads of yellow snakes, dissatisfied and bitter.

She slid her feet across the floor, hoping they would make way for her passing body. Some did, but some were caught under her feet and began to die. Naamah crouched and swept her arm across the floor to make a space for herself. She sat with her legs crossed, watching the wall ahead of her morph and distort. If she unfocused her eyes, the shapes seemed to move toward her. The wall would bend and lean, veer in a blink of her eye.

She closed her eyes and tried to feel the movement in her body, too, which she knew should be its own collection of endless contortions. She felt nothing but steady. She turned and pushed aside more moths so she might lie down. On her back, the moths began to climb her. She ignored them. She knew she could feel the unreliability of her own form if she could only figure out how. She tried not to focus on her body. She tried to will herself into motion. She tried to feel the floor move beneath her. And then suddenly it worked. She felt it move, and her body, in staying still, felt such a jolt that she screamed.

The moths weren't bothered at all.

NOAH TELLS Naamah that one lamb is doing better than the other. Naamah, determined to prevent another outburst from one of the large predators, decides to feed the weaker lamb to a tiger who's been showing signs of hunger. Since what happened to Shem, she's been spending more time than she'd like to admit outside the predators' rooms, hovering outside in the early mornings, listening as they pace and scratch, bellies grumbling.

Sadie is there when Naamah goes to get the lamb.

"Oh," Naamah says, "I didn't realize anyone was in here."

"That's okay, Naamah. Would you like to sit with me?"

Naamah nods and plops down right where she is, by the door.

Sadie smiles at her. "These little ones give me such joy." The lambs spring about. Over to Naamah and back again. Naamah can hear their hooves pop, pop, popping. She feels one starting to nibble at her pocket, where she's stuffed a bit of clover she brought from the garden on the deck. She reaches down and can tell it's the larger lamb. It must be. But the treat is for the smaller lamb, the sacrifice, and Naamah pushes the lamb away.

"Where is the little one?" she asks Sadie.

Sadie grabs hold of him and pulls him over to Naamah. "That was sweet of you to bring," Sadie says, gesturing at the clover.

Naamah gets down on her knees, takes him in her arms, and brings the clover under his chin. "No, Sadie. It wasn't." Naamah can't look at her. "I have to take him. The tiger could become dangerous."

Sadie's eyes fill with tears.

Naamah says, "It's just . . . the water isn't going down fast enough. You know that."

Sadie still doesn't respond.

"It's not the first time we've had to. I . . ."

The sheep begin to bleat, as if they know.

"I wanted to shield you from it."

"How often have you done it?" Sadie asks.

"Not terribly often."

"You're lying to me, Naamah."

Naamah looks at her. "Please, let me." She looks down again. "Let me this time."

Sadie stands, brushes hay off her dress. Tears are falling down her cheeks, but she doesn't whimper as she leaves the room. Naamah waits until she can't hear Sadie's footsteps. Then she picks up the lamb.

FOR THREE DAYS IN A ROW, Naamah returned to the room with the moths. On the second day, she spent hours examining them, scouring their bodies, and she discovered they had no mouths. She tried to entice them with food, to provoke some proboscis to unfurl. When she finally accepted that there was nothing to find, she thought, *Well, how long can they live like this?*

On the third day, almost all of them were dead. Their bodies were piled in layers on the floor. Some clung dead to the walls. She brought in the largest bag she could find, and started to gather up the moths. Their wings did not hold their shape at her touch. Some structural piece—inside them, around them, she didn't know—broke, but nothing broke off. She grabbed them by the handful, threw body after body into the bag. She let the bag hang open like a mouth and swept them in by the armful. When the bag was full enough to stand on its own, she arranged its open mouth and tried to scoop them in. They fell between her elbows, slipped down against her body. Then she took the bag to the room of snakes, to the lizards, the birds, the monkeys, and spent a whole day treating animals to the spoils of the room.

DESPITE SADIE'S DISTRESS, Naamah finds herself outside the door of the tiger's room feeling oddly indifferent. She feels the lamb's quick breath and beating heart under her arm and against her own chest, and she wonders if it would be kinder to kill him before she takes him in. *Of course it would be.* She kneels down, places the lamb beside her, and breaks its neck over her leg. Then she tosses the dead body into the tiger's feeding room and closes the door loudly behind her. *Why is this any different than the moths?* she asks herself over and over.

WHEN SHE'D CLEARED THE ROOM of dead moths, she found the thousands of eggs they'd left behind. She decided to kill almost all of them, then and there. She scraped them off the floor, gathered them in a bucket, took them to the deck, and threw them in the water. When the remaining eggs hatched, she fed many of the caterpillars to the other animals, just as she had done with the moths. She left about fifty caterpillars to do the process all over again. She feared that if she left only a few, she might sense their genders subconsciously and select only female caterpillars to save. Then they'd never exist on earth again; she'd never again have a room that could change everything she knew about how she could exist inside a space. In the days that followed, she saw the pattern of the moths everywhere, even when she looked at the sky. The world felt smaller because of this, her body more at ease.

# EIGHT

Noah finds Naamah lying next to the garden, her chin resting on the top of the frame, her fingers gently on top of the leaves of the clover.

"The ewe is rejecting the lamb," he says.

She raises her head off the wood.

"Will you come?"

"Yes," she says, and they go to the room of sheep. Inside, he forgets that she can't see them until she reminds him by clearing her throat.

"Right," he says, going over to the ewe. "Here she is. And"— stretching over and dragging the lamb toward him—"here's the lamb."

The ewe kicks at the lamb, and Noah jumps back, shuffling the lamb farther away. Naamah spots some of the lamb's shit. "Rub this on the ewe's nose and the lamb's butt."

He does what she says.

"Now, shove the lamb toward her teat, and with luck she'll bend around to smell the lamb."

"You think this will work?"

"Not really."

"Wha—why?"

"Because she's not really rejecting the lamb. She's depressed about the other lamb, and I don't blame her. And now I bet she's in pain, too, swollen with enough milk for two lambs. Well, almost two."

Noah looks at Naamah.

"Is she still right here?"

"Yes," he says, and he moves her hand to the dam's back.

She leans down and whispers into her neck. "Please. Please, take her back." She stays there with her face in the dirty wool.

"Are you okay, Naamah?"

She shakes her head. "Did I do the right thing?"

"Yes," he says, "you did."

She's still shaking her head in the wool.

"Where was that lamb going to live?" he asks, and he picks her up off the dam and tries to look her in the eyes. "Where, Naamah? There's no land out there yet. There's just water."

"I know."

"And it's done. What's done is done. We can't change it now."

She buries her head in his chest. "But you wouldn't change it, right? If we could?"

"I wouldn't change it."

"Okay," Naamah says.

"Okay." Noah strokes her hair. "Are you ready to get back to this?"

She nods.

But no matter what they try, they can't make it right with the dam.

———

TEN WEEKS AFTER the moths died, her magical room was back again. But it wasn't like before. Sitting and staring at the wall, she could think only of their impending deaths, the bag of broken wings, how brashly she would have to work to clear the room again.

And then that day was upon her. As she was carrying the full bag down the hall, she ran into Neela, coming out of a room Naamah had never noticed.

"What's in there, Neela?"

"Nothing." Neela blushed.

"Come on, which animal?" Naamah couldn't imagine why she'd blushed, unless she'd been watching animals have sex, or some other thing that women blush about.

"No, there's—"

Naamah pushed through her and opened the door herself. She could feel Neela standing behind her, not embarrassed or nervous, but watching to see her reaction. *Is my reaction such an unknown?* Naamah thought. *Aren't I the most predictable thing?*

The room was full of paintings, canvases stretched over wooden frames. Naamah walked slowly through the room. They were organized into landscapes, abstracts, still lifes, portraits. At the portraits, Naamah's eyes stung. There was a painting of Sadie's younger sisters, one on the lap of the other, sitting patiently under an acacia tree.

"Does Sadie know about this?"

Neela shook her head.

"Good." She wiped her eyes. "Did you paint these?"

"Some of them," she said. "I was worried. I was worried we wouldn't have art anymore."

"Now we will." Naamah turned and took Neela's head in her hands, brought it down, and kissed her on her forehead. "Thank you," she said, and then she went back to feed the bodies of moths to the animals who would make the world bountiful again.

NAAMAH FEELS she has to save the lamb, or the ewe. Or maybe it's the broken bond she wants to save. When she goes to check on them, the room smells of mint. Noah's flat hand is rubbing an empty space low in the air that she knows must be an udder. If that doesn't fix it, the udder could become infected. Naamah slips back out of the room without Noah noticing.

She slides the ladder down, climbs down to the little island, and goes into the water.

"I haven't seen you in a while," the angel says when Naamah reaches her. The village she's built has gotten bigger. Hallways of crystal arches extend in all directions, like roads through a valley. They seem to go on forever, but really they go only as far as Naamah can see.

"You know Shem was hurt," Naamah says.

"Yes."

"He's okay."

"Good," the angel says.

"And then a ewe had two lambs."

"That's good, too, isn't it?"

"No. I mean, yes. But no. One wasn't doing well, so I fed it to a tiger. I killed it and fed it to a tiger. And now the dam won't feed the other one. And she's got a clogged milk duct, and it could get worse. Everything could get worse, I think."

The angel swims into a shimmering room. "If these two sheep die, what will happen?"

"Nothing." But then she corrects herself. "Well, a bigger animal will be fed."

"Then why do you care? Why are you here?"

"I need your help. I want them to live."

"But that's not up to you."

"I mean, it's kind of up to me."

"Naamah."

"What? Come on. You're down here, creating a world for dead people. Don't tell me."

"Naamah!"

"You're all like, *The angel said, Let the waters bring forth abundantly the moving creature that hath death, bring them below the earth in the drowned firmament of angel-heaven.*"

"Fuck you."

"Oh, can you say that?" Naamah says.

"Yes, I can say that."

"You know, because I just wasn't sure."

"I get it," the angel says dryly.

"Like, is *He* still your father?"

"Shut up now, Naamah."

"I mean, what *can* you do?"

"I can do whatever the fuck I want, and you know that."

"So come help me save a damn sheep."

"Two sheep."

"Two damn sheep."

The angel swims once around the room. "Do you have a plan?"

"Can you make yourself invisible?"

"No."

"Then come tonight."

"I don't care about these sheep, Naamah."

"But you care about me for some reason. So come to the boat."

"Why not ask me for help? Why antagonize me? What have I done to upset you?"

"Just come to the boat," Naamah says.

AFTER FINDING Neela's room of art, Naamah was overcome by thoughts of other inanimate objects she hadn't thought to save. Conch shells. Pottery. They'd all had a little jewelry, a few pieces, but they'd made no attempt to buy anything exceptional before the flood. Money had seemed worthless, knowing what would come. She wasn't sure she could remember the last time she'd even caught her own reflection in something that shined, something that was not the plain surface of water.

In her bedroom, Naamah ran her fingers through her hair. It felt nice. She wondered what it looked like to have her fingers out of sight, hidden in her hair. Probably nothing spectacular. What would be spectacular is if she pulled her hand away and she had no fingers. What would be spectacular is if her hair were crawling with fingers. Fingers pale as maggots. Fingers dark as the hair they were in.

Noah walked in and sat behind her in the bed. He moved his fingers up under her hair, up to the top of her skull. She hummed a sigh and lay down beside him. He bent over her and took her head in his hands, ran his thumbs over her forehead, starting them at the top of her nose and then over her eyebrows. Then he pressed his thumbs under her eyebrows, then on the ridge of her nose, then under her cheekbones, push by push, following the cheekbones to the joints of the jaw.

He dragged his thumbs down her jawline and her mouth slacked open. She remembered the first time he massaged her face, how she'd felt embarrassment at her mouth agape and breathing hot. But not anymore. He paused above her chin, below her bottom lip, pressing again.

"Good?" he asked.

She nodded, almost asleep.

He put his hands on either side of her head, lowered his forehead to hers, and then rolled off to fall asleep beside her.

# NINE

In the middle of the night, Naamah goes to the deck to wait. As the angel comes out of the water, as her black skin touches the air, she is alight, as if she'd been another thing dampened by the water. But the brightness of her form renders her slightly out of focus just the same.

"Thank you for coming," Naamah says.

"You're welcome," says the angel, and then she runs her hand down Naamah's arm, letting Naamah take her hand.

Naamah leads her to the room with the sheep. The angel goes over to the dam. The angel doesn't bend over—she doesn't even look down—but by the shape of her hands, Naamah can tell she's holding the dam's head. Then she lets go of the head and walks back to Naamah.

"That's it?" Naamah asks.

"Yes."

"How?"

"I made her forget."

"You what?"

"I made her forget the first lamb."

Naamah starts to cry. "How could you do that?"

"How did you think this was going to work?"

"I don't know. I thought you could make her feel better. Show her the little lamb in the heavens or something."

"Of all people, Naamah, you should know how little comfort there is in that."

"You could have made her feel committed to the child she has left."

"This was easier."

Naamah wipes her eyes with her wrists. "Can you undo it?"

The angel stares at her.

"Can you put it back? Her love of the little lamb?"

"I could, but I won't. She will die. The healthy lamb will die."

"You don't know that."

"I do."

Naamah can't look at her.

"I'll leave it to you," the angel finally says. "I'll put it back if you want. And the remaining two will die. Which do you prefer?"

"Leave it," Naamah says, so quietly that the angel can barely hear her.

"You still can't see them?" the angel asks.

Naamah shakes her head.

"You don't have to stay here. You can stay with me," the angel says, putting her hand on Naamah's arm again.

"You said I can't. You said it would draw too much attention to yourself."

"I'm changing my mind," the angel says.

"No. It doesn't matter. I can't leave."

"Why not?"

"I have my sons," Naamah says.

"I can tell how much they mean to you," the angel says. "I can make you forget, too."

Naamah steps back from her. "Don't say that," she says. "Don't ever say that."

MANY NIGHTS, Naamah would fall asleep with the fat of Noah's hand between her back teeth, sometimes his last knuckle. It kept her from clenching her jaw as she fell asleep. She never knew when during the night she let go.

For months, when Ham was a toddler, he fell asleep with his fingers in Naamah's mouth. He'd put them there when he was nursing and then close his eyes, sleeping that way longer and longer each night. Or he'd wake her in the middle of the night by sticking his fingers in her mouth, and that would settle him back to sleep again.

Once Ham finished breastfeeding, Naamah put him into bed with the other boys. They all slept together. And sometimes she'd come into the room after they were asleep, after she'd swept the mess they'd left where they'd eaten, and Ham's small fingers would be in Japheth's mouth, or on Japheth's cheek after he'd turned his head.

If a scorpion found its way into their home, Naamah would bang it dead with a metal pot, and only Shem and Noah would wake. Noah would ask if everything was okay and then fall back to sleep. Shem would say something absurd, like, "Mommy, I was underwater." *Wait, is that right?* Shem always used to have dreams about being underwater. *Yes.* Then he would lie back down and be asleep again, too.

How had she forgotten?

IN THE MORNING, Adata finds Naamah looking out over the water and walks over to her. "It looks like the lamb is doing well."

"Yes," Naamah says, not turning to her.

"I was glad to see that."

"Yes, me too."

"Are things okay with us?" Adata asks.

"Yes."

"But you can't look at me?"

"I can," Naamah says, keeping her eyes on the water.

"When I look at you, I think about your mouth, but I still look at you."

"You"—she's unsure if she should finish—"are one woman of many, Adata."

"I was, wasn't I?" Adata says.

Despite herself, Naamah laughs. She turns herself around and leans back on the railing. "Do you get no pleasure from sex with Japheth?"

"We haven't had sex yet. Because of the ark. But I've had sex with men before. I get little pleasure from it."

"Are you attracted to Japheth?"

"He's a handsome man, Naamah."

"No, I'm not asking as a mother."

"Then no."

"Do you think you can make him feel attractive?"

"Yes, I think I can. Maybe not in ways he'd expect, but I can."

Naamah turns back to the water.

"What about you?" Adata asks. "Are you attracted to Noah?"

"Very much so. I always have been."

"And also to women?"

"Yes, though I discovered that later."

"I've known since I was seven," Adata says.

"I only have a few memories of my childhood anymore."

"Tell me one."

Naamah closes her eyes. "I wanted my mother to lift me up, but she was pregnant and couldn't lift me over her big belly."

"That's it?"

Naamah laughs. "It's the oldest memory I have. I think I was three."

"Who was in her belly?"

"My brother. He died when I was young. When he was young."

"Still a child?"

"Yes."

"I'm sorry."

"My favorite memory of him was one night, after a dinner when we'd both eaten too much, stayed at the table longer than anyone. And we lifted up our shirts to show each other how much we'd eaten, how stuffed we were. I poked his belly and he felt mine, and he said, 'I wish I could feel your bones.' And we laughed so hard."

"He sounds like Shem."

"Yes! Yes, he was a lot like Shem. I haven't thought about him in a long time."

"Were both your parents dead before the flood?"

"Yes."

"What was the name of the woman you loved?"

"Bethel."

"I think that means *the house of God*."

Naamah laughs.

"What did she look like?"

Naamah shook her head.

"Like me?"

"No, not like you. You look like you work, like your hands are rough with working. She looked like she never worked, like she never had to pull her hair back, like she never even needed to wash her hands, even though she did work sometimes."

"She sounds lovely."

Naamah nodded.

"A good place to worship."

Naamah smiled at her, the biggest smile Adata had ever seen on her face. Unlike Naamah's laugh, which nearly shut her eyes, her smile left her eyes large and sparkling in the sun, as if two golden beetles had been living there all along, flashing back and forth to black, waiting for moments in the sun like this, at the edge of the boat.

# TEN

In this dream, Naamah is somewhere very cold. In every direction there is snow on the ground and in the sky.

"Naamah."

She looks up. "Hello, Jael." It feels good to be able to see him.

"You could not find me," he says. "I found you. It's my dream! I knew it."

"Aren't you cold, Jael?"

"Yes."

She lifts up a fold in her clothing, near her chest. He lands on her hand and lets her lead him under the cloth, so that one of his wings is against her chest. He can still look ahead of them, wherever they are going. "If this is your dream, what are we doing here?"

"That I don't know," Jael says. "I'd never come here. Would you?"

"No."

"Maybe it's not either of our dreams."

"Probably not," Naamah says.

She keeps walking forward. She can't make out anything around her. Soon she feels a pain in her shins and she knows she's walking up a hill. She hasn't walked up a steep hill in a long time. The steps and ladders and ramps on the ship aren't like this.

When she reaches the top of the hill, she stops and the snow stops, too. Below her, the snow tapers into ice banks and water. The water is calm the way the floodwaters are calm.

The longer she stands there, the more animals reveal themselves: arctic foxes, arctic dolphins, arctic loons, polar bears, penguins, ivory gulls, snowy owls, little auks, even an arctic whale. With their movement, each flapping wing, each dolphin's spout, they make the place look vibrant, even though they're only a dozen shades of white. Still, it's quiet.

"Damn," Jael says.

"Really," Naamah says.

"What do they all eat?" he asks.

"Each other, I guess."

As they stand there and watch, the animals begin to behave strangely. The whales and dolphins begin lobtailing, and the sounds their flukes make against the water are loud as they echo against the banks of ice, the hills of snow. And then their bodies rise out of the water as if their flukes were wings and their noses were pointed toes poised on the water.

Then the birds, all the birds, start flying into the giant flanks of the whales and dolphins and fall into the water. Eventually the birds begin to break the skins of the animals, until the bodies are spotted with blood.

When the penguins appear again, they each have two heads. The foxes have human ears. The polar bears are disfigured, with short back legs that cannot bend, and they drag their lopsided bodies behind them.

A hush falls across the scene and the upside-down whales open their mouths wide and their bodies fall down through them into the water. When they jump back out, their bodies are inside out, the grotesqueness of their muscular and cardiovascular systems laid bare.

The spectacle of it is magnificent, but Naamah retches.

"Watch the feathers," Jael says. He squirms out from his warm spot on her chest.

"Sorry."

"I bet, if I focus really hard, I can get us out of here," he says.

"Okay," Naamah says, breathing hard and shaking.

He lands on the back of her shoulder and raises his wings over his eyes. Nothing happens. He lowers his wings in a huff. "It's not working."

"No."

"Well, you try something."

She rights herself, takes a deep breath, but still feels like she's shaking. She closes her eyes, and with another deep breath she understands she is not shaking but buzzing. She feels like she's going to explode.

"Jael! Off!"

He flies high into the air, and she opens her mouth. Thousands of bees pour out from within her, overtaking every gruesome animal in the arctic scene. Every animal turns brown, like mustard seeds, the bees' transparent wings sending off little glints. Every animal is given a new, very busy skin.

Jael comes back down to Naamah's shoulder as they watch together.

The bees make quick work of the bodies of the animals, and as
they do, the bodies become even more misshapen than they already
were, folding in on themselves. Soon the animals are down to skele-
tons, some clinging to one tough organ. In one bear, the bees eat its
hanging heart from within, the muscle glistening like an oil slick
shaking on water.

Naamah retches again.

Afraid that the bees will come back to her when they're finished,
she leaves, running away. Jael is startled off her shoulder and follows
her in flight. Naamah hears each flap of his wings in the cold air.

"Where are you going?" he asks.

"I don't know how long we will be here. We need shelter."

She runs until they come to a snowdrift formed by what must
have been a harsher wind in the storm that blinded them before. She
starts to dig down at the edge of the small hill of snow. When the
snow reaches her knees, she starts to dig forward into the hill.

This should all take a long time. She should be exhausted and
sweating and then nervous about sweating in the cold. But the work
is easy and soon the cave is built.

"This is nice," says Jael.

Naamah nods, settling in, trying not to be unnerved by her
strength in the dream.

"Do you think I might be filled with carnivorous bees, too?"
he asks.

"Does it feel like you are?"

"No." Jael pauses. "Did it feel like you were?"

"Yes. Just before it happened."

"You wiped out all those animals."

"I know," she says.

"I can't tell if I feel bad about that," he says.

"Let's talk about something else. I don't want to throw up in here."

In the cave, the air is beginning to feel warm and thick. If Jael stopped talking, Naamah would surely fall asleep.

"I miss trees," he says.

"Me too." She's nodding off anyway.

Jael comes back to her chest and she folds him up.

WHEN THEY FALL ASLEEP, Naamah wakes in her bed with Noah. He is just out of reach, too far for her to lay her hand on his chest, to feel his heartbeat. And his breath is silent, or quieter than the other noises of the boat. But the room and the bed are warm, so she knows he's alive, and that's enough. She falls back to sleep.

IN THE DREAM, she's in a block of ice now, standing upright, float-ing in the arctic waters. Jael is on top of the block. She can't see him, but she can hear his talons scratching.

"Naamah! Can you hear me? I will get you out of this."

But Naamah's not in danger. She's not cold. She can breathe. She thinks she may be strong enough in this dream to break out of the ice whenever she chooses. So she chooses to enjoy it, since she'll never be in this odd position again.

The ice doesn't bob in the water. It floats straight on. The ice and her body are mostly beneath the surface. Her head admires the line of the still water and the near-perfect reflections it offers to every crest of snow.

Sometimes she catches a glimpse of what's below the water, like a school of fish. But eventually she tires of moving the way a boat would. She raises her shoulders and the ice lurches up and begins to crack. It bobs. Jael flies above it. She feels sick again. She pushes her toes down and the ice cracks more, so much so that capillaries of water creep into the ice.

She raises her shoulders and pushes her toes down at the same time and the ice splits along a crack above her shoulders. She kicks and the ice breaks up around her feet, but she's left with a giant ice block on her head, still floating her along. Jael flies back down and slams his beak into the ice.

Naamah pounds on it with her fists from below, as best she can, dragging her fists through the water. Even so, it's working. The ice cracks thinly at first, and on another pound, the cracks double in size, refiguring themselves into the shape of a tree's broad branches, until all the ice between the branches falls away in chunks.

Then Naamah is only a body again and she has to swim to stay afloat and alive in the water.

"Are you okay?" Jael asks.

Naamah twists onto her back and wiggles her hands back and forth under the water at her waist, and she watches Jael above her. "Yes," she says.

"Aren't you cold?"

"No."

"Look." Jael motions.

Naamah flips back over and sees a group of seals on an iceberg. She swims to it and climbs on. Her elbows and wrists feel strange next to the fins of the seals; she's making such a show of her angles.

She lies down between the seals. They're soft and warm and smooth, and she's not sure how they will take to her petting them, but she pets one anyway. She has to believe they can recognize a gesture of adoration and comfort. And though the seal does recognize her intent, it is not comforted. The seals feel unusual for the first time in their lives, beside this body of a human who's so transfixed by them. And unusual feels unsafe.

One seal starts to bark at her and, to move her off the ice, slowly, bumps her away. The others raise their heads up, add their barks to the chorus. Naamah thinks she sees the Metatron perched behind them all, his striking yellow head.

"Okay, okay," Naamah says, and she slides back off the ice into the water. But this time she can do nothing to stay afloat. She sinks farther and farther down. It takes only seconds before she can't see Jael above her. Everything she sees turns that dusty navy blue, as if she is disappearing into Jael instead of the water.

The same soft film forms over her mouth. "This is all a little too familiar, don't you think? A little too convenient!" she yells.

But here her words push out the film into a bubble around her whole body. She screams as loud and long as she can, and once the bubble is large, she falls to the bottom of it with a plop. She sits there, steady in the water. The bubble doesn't seem to be moving at all.

An octopus approaches the bubble. It grabs onto it and moves down to where Naamah sits. She lies down on her stomach to be closer to the octopus, who has tilted its grinning black eye toward Naamah's round face. Then it starts to bite at the bubble with its beak.

When the beak recedes, it reminds Naamah of a baby boy's penis, receding into the fat pads boys are often born with. When she pushed her boys' foreskins back, to clean the heads of their penises, the urethras opened slightly, like the mouths of the smallest fish. As the boys grew older, they grew into their circumcisions. The heads of their penises hung under the shafts.

With Naamah's hand against the bubble, she can feel the suckers along the octopus's tentacles. She closes her eyes to its penis-mouth and moves her hand back and forth over the two rows of suckers, counting them to herself, hopping between rows.

Soon the octopus grows tired of her and the bubble and starts to leave.

"Wait!" Naamah says. "Give me a shove?"

As the octopus twists away, it swings all eight tentacles at the bubble and launches the bubble toward the surface. When Naamah reaches the surface, she's no longer in the arctic. All the water is gone, and she's back in the desert again. The bubble pops.

Sarai is there, on her throne. "Naamah," she says, "so good to see you."

"You've said that to me before."

"It's still true."

"But why do you keep saying it to me?"

"I married Abraham. He is descended from Shem. Seeing you is like seeing a mother, or a grandmother."

Naamah walks up to her now, right up to her face, planning to say, *What does that mean to me?* But she does feel connected to her, and also taken with the sight of her. She says, "You're so beautiful."

"Thank you," Sarai says, used to this reaction.

"How distantly are we related?" Naamah asks.

"Very. But we spoke of you often, told the story of your sacrifices."

"Is that how you speak of it? Sacrifices?"

"Yes."

"Not as something righteous?"

"That too."

"How do *you* think of it?" Naamah asks her.

"I am only grateful. If it weren't for you, I would not have my son."

"Where is he now?"

"He's dead. No . . ." She corrects herself. "At this point in time, he hasn't been born."

"This point in time, here in the dream?"

Sarai nods.

"How are you here?"

"The women in our family, Naamah, they've been powerful for a long time. When I died, I found I could move through time as I wished. But so far I have largely stayed in dreams, where I can interact with people, where I can create things like this throne, where I can sit and watch the desert."

"Is this your dream?" Jael asks Sarai. He's back, and Naamah is relieved to see him. He swoops down and lands on Naamah's shoulder.

"No, I think this is Naamah's dream, mostly."

Naamah rubs the back of Jael's head with her bent fingers.

"What is a righteous thing worth?" Naamah asks.

"It's worth lives," Sarai answers.

"It *costs* lives," Naamah says.

"Then its worth is impossible to discuss, for lives cannot be measured against other lives."

"Do you think God would think this?"

Sarai is silent for a long time. Then she says, "He ordered my husband to kill my son."

"A child of mine?"

Sarai nods.

"What happened?"

"He said, 'Take your son, your only son, whom you love—Isaac—and go to the region of Moriah. Sacrifice him there as a burnt offering on a mountain I will show you.'"

Naamah draws Jael closer to her.

"It wasn't true. He had another son, Ishmael, with my handmaiden, Hagar. He loved Ishmael, too. I wondered if that made it easier for him to take Isaac to the mountain as he did."

"Have you ever spoken to God?"

"No, but I have heard him speak to Abraham, in the voices of three men who came once to our tent."

"I'm sorry—that's not really what I want to know. What happened to Isaac?"

"It's okay. You're scared. To hear the story told straight through, it is scary. Should I tell you now that Isaac was not killed?"

"Yes." Naamah tries to relax her jaw. "That helps."

"Abraham took him, with donkeys and servants, to find the

mountain. And days later they found the mountain, and he set out farther, with only Isaac and the supplies for the altar. It is difficult to tell you this, to recall it all. It's been so long since I remembered."

"Remembered what?"

"That God didn't say to Abraham that he had to make our son carry the wood he would be sacrificed on, and yet Abraham made him do this."

Naamah pulls in a breath.

"Abraham built the altar, arranged the wood, and laid our son down on that wood, which had already spent time pressed to his small back. And then Abraham grabbed his knife. He got that far."

Naamah tries to take her hand to offer her some comfort, but Sarai raises it away from Naamah and shakes her head.

"An angel of God called out to my husband and said, 'Do not lay a hand on the boy.' And instead of running from that place with our son, he stayed and sacrificed a ram and let the angel continue on about His promises to our people." Sarai presses her thumbnail into the knuckle of her forefinger. "Then they came home to me, changed men both, having heard the angel of the Lord, some sort of joy on their faces, some pride.

"In Isaac I recognized a restlessness with regard to the size of his life. I could relate to that. Not because my life felt small and strange within the grandness of God, but because my life felt large when everyone else saw me as small and inept. And perhaps I was inept." She begins to cry, but her back doesn't bend away from the throne. "Perhaps I was, Naamah, for such a thing to befall my son. For God to think He could make this threat against me and my family."

Sarai wipes away her tears and looks as she did before. Composed again, she says, "God cannot be judged because He cannot be understood."

"I judge Him just the same," Naamah says.

"Maybe I did, too, when I was alive. I know from my travels that we are not the last women to do so."

"But you do not judge Him now?"

"Today I judge myself. I don't know who I will judge tomorrow. What will you do tomorrow?"

"I will wake up again on the boat."

"How nice it is, then"—Sarai smiles at them—"to be with me now, here."

## ELEVEN

Before the sun rises, Naamah goes to the bucket of wood ash they keep in the hall. She takes a cup, dips it in, brings up just enough ash to cover the bottom of the cup. On the deck she prepares a bath, adds water to the cup with ashes, and mixes it with her finger. She places it on the edge of the bath and gets in. She scrubs her skin with a cloth.

She rubs and grabs at her pubic hairs, pulling free any that have fallen out. She holds up her hand, hairs clinging to it—some because they've curled around her fingers, some because everything is wet. *Is this something every woman has experienced?* she thinks. *Is this a sight every woman has seen?* She dips her hand back into the water and the hairs let go. She sees them floating in the water, but one is on top of it, showing the shine of the water where it puckers its nearly-there skin.

She drops her head back and then lifts it again, heavy and dripping. Then she takes the cup of water, thickened with ash, and pours it onto her head, lathers it into her hair. She takes a long time rubbing it in, down to the scalp, before she leans back again. When the water creeps over her hairline, she moves her head back and forth. She runs her hands from her forehead back, until her hair feels like it's free of ash.

The sun is rising, and Naamah turns her head to watch it. That's when she sees something she hasn't seen in months: the horizon, interrupted. She jumps out of the bath and runs to the railing. The mountaintops are out. A whole mountain range, all the peaks, starting close to the boat and stretching out as far as she can see, scattered through the water like a path, the kind of path a child might hop along, a giant child, God.

Naamah gets dressed and finds Japheth first. She wants to take a mountain goat out on a little boat to one of the drying peaks.

"Shouldn't we tell the others?" Japheth says.

"It's so early," she says, "and the mountaintops aren't going anywhere."

So Japheth gets her a mountain goat, and they clamber onto a boat. He rows while she pets the goat she cannot see. She can feel its short hair falling out in her fingers.

"Their eyes are odd," he says, "like their pupils are winking at me."

"I remember," she says, picturing them. She's reminded of an octopus's eye, but she's not sure why. She's not sure how she even knows what an octopus's eye looks like.

At the mountaintop, she stays in the boat while Japheth carries the goat above the water and sets him down on the rock of it. Then he returns to the boat, where he wrings out his clothes. She listens to the goat scamper about on the peak.

"It's a nice day," Japheth says.

Naamah nods and smiles at him, but it's easier to pass the time without speaking. She lies back, closes her eyes, and takes in the sun while listening to the goat's hooves.

Eventually the goat gets tired of the mountaintop. He cries out a few times, and it sounds like someone is calling for her from far away. But before Japheth makes it out of the boat, the goat starts to swim back to them. He's drenched when Japheth pulls him over the side. Naamah sees the drops of water hitting the wood.

"Even he knows nothing's ready," Naamah says.

"Yes," Japheth says, and he rows them all back to the boat, which looms nearby, bigger than any of the mountaintops for now.

Not sure how long she will have access to the angel and the village of dead, Naamah starts to visit them every day. She has to wade farther and farther out before she can dive down.

On the first day, the children ask to see her legs. "What's that?" a girl asks.

"Bruises. Do you remember those?"

The children shake their heads.

"Are they always in that shape?"

"No, a dog jumped on my thigh, and this is the paw print. See? The pad of the foot and the four toes?"

"Can I touch it?"

Naamah nods.

The girl touches it, outlines it. "I can't feel it," she says.

"It's underneath the skin."

"What is?"

"The injury, I guess."

"Does it hurt?"

"Only when it's touched."

The girl snaps her hand away. "I'm sorry."

"No, no. You'd have to touch it harder. And even then, it's only a little soreness."

"What is being sore like?"

"It's an ache. Or like being stiff when you wake up. Do you sleep?"

"Yes."

"Do you ever feel stiff?" Naamah reaches up her arms. "Like you want to stretch?" She bends to the left and right.

The children giggle, and they all mimic her. She looks at them all swaying in the water like the spirits they are.

THE NEXT DAY, the children ask to see the bruises on her leg again. The paw print is a different color, more green.

"Will you grow something here?"

"What do you mean?" Naamah asks.

"Like a plant."

"No," she says. "It changes as it heals. Next it will be more yellow."

"Like little suns?"

"Yes, but it will look too sourly yellow to be the sun."

The children pull at her toes.

"Do you remember the sun?" she asks.

"Yes," the children say excitedly. "We've made a story about the sun."

"Have you?"

They nod.

"Can I hear it?"

"The sun hid when the rain came. It went to another world where there was no rain and never would be rain. But then, by accident, the sun burned the new world and said, *I'm sorry, I'm sorry.* The new world did not forgive the sun, so the sun came back here."

"I love that story," Naamah says. "That's a very good story."

THE NEXT DAY, the children have prepared a play for Naamah. The angel has designed a stage and costumes for each of them. A child comes out in the shape of the sun as children imagine it: a perfectly symmetrical, far-reaching thing, with beams of light zigzagging out of it.

"I am so bored," the sun-child says. "Look at the animals here. Look at these children running around. Haven't I seen this before? I have. I have."

The rest of the children run around in front of her.

"I will go somewhere else and see something new."

The children leave and the sun-child walks in a circle, returning to center stage, as a child dressed as a planet comes from stage right.

"Wow," says the sun-child, looking at the new planet.

From offstage, a child yells, "Meanwhile, back on Earth!"

The sun runs off, and the rest of the children come back dressed as raindrops. "Boom!" they yell as they stomp around the stage. "Boom boom boom!" The children try not to laugh as they run into each other. And then they run off again.

The sun-child and planet-child come back. "Ow!" says the planet-child. "You burned me."

"I'm sorry! I didn't mean to!"

"I want you to leave!"

The sun-child starts to circle the stage again, and all the raindrop-children come back. When the sun-child is at the very back of the stage, Naamah can see only the top of her zigzagging beams of crystal light. She comes center stage by passing through the raindrop-children, and they all dramatically peel away, left and right. Some groan in defeat.

"The world looks different now." The sun-child looks around. "What is different?" She looks at Naamah. "What is different?"

Naamah's cheeks feel hot. "All the children are gone."

"Yes! That's it! And all this water in their place. What a different world now. I will stay here until the water is gone. At least until then."

The children offstage are shaking off their raindrop costumes; the shattering pieces of crystal float down in the water. Then they run back onstage.

"Oh yes, please stay."

"Please stay, sun."

"We are so happy when you're here."

"And alive!" shouts a young child.

All the children fall silent.

Naamah can't tell if that was the ending of the play, as they had planned it, but she tries to clap. But trying to clap in the water is foolish, so she throws up her arms, hollers and cheers. "What a great play! Wonderfully done, children! Wonderful!"

The children take their bows.

THE NEXT DAY, the angel asks Naamah what she's doing here.

"I could ask you the same," Naamah says.

The angel's quiet.

"Where else could you be?" Naamah asks. "The heavens. The underworld. But could you be anywhere else if you wanted? In another world, like the sun in the children's play?"

"Yes."

"Do you ever mention God to them?"

"No."

"What would happen to them if you leave?"

"Nothing. They can stay. They can leave."

"Really? You think everything would just continue."

"Yes."

"Then why not leave, get out of here?"

The angel's quiet again.

"It's for me, isn't it? That's why you're still here," Naamah says.

The angel looks at her.

"What do you want from me?" Naamah gets in her face. "What do you want?"

The angel kisses Naamah, and Naamah pulls back and floats away in the water. The angel waits for her, and she's right to. Naamah returns to her. When she takes the angel's tongue in her mouth, the film between them is gone.

WHEN NAAMAH AND NOAH were first together, there were times she would take his penis into her mouth. And even when she rounded her lips over her teeth, she still felt her back teeth touch the edge of the head of his penis. Her body felt mismatched to his, but she knew, from having taken other men's penises into her mouth, that this was true with any penis. And really it was a feeling about her own body—that she was misusing it, misunderstanding it. She never felt that with her tongue inside a woman's vagina.

Still, on a man, she liked playing with the point where the edge of the head gathered toward the tip. But sometimes Noah could not resist moving his hips. And then her body felt wrong again—his speed not meant to be mirrored by her neck. So she would stand up, and he would lift her by her thighs and place her on him. She would control the speed with which she fell down the shaft of his penis, how much slack she allowed in her hips until she reached his soft hair.

If she had to decide which part of sex with Noah she liked best, it would be his strength.

But once or twice he ejaculated in her mouth, and his semen made her mouth crawl, and there wasn't enough water to rinse it out, there wasn't enough bread to chew into a paste that would finally turn sweet.

———————

THE ANGEL GRABS AT Naamah's body and Naamah grabs back. Naamah's arms settle along the sides of the angel's head, her hands in her hair. The angel hoists Naamah high, with her hands tight on her ass, and Naamah's legs wrap around her. Naamah doesn't know if the angel has enormous strength or if the water makes all the difference.

If they were in the desert, Naamah thinks, the angel would throw her down on the bed next. Instead, the angel keeps lifting her, dragging her top teeth down Naamah's stomach. Naamah feels weightless. She has to link her legs around the angel's head to keep from drifting away. The angel flicks her tongue over her clit faster than anyone ever has. Soon Naamah has ejaculated, but she hasn't orgasmed. She wonders if the angel can find the spot that Bethel found with precision, that Noah's penis finds bluntly every time.

It's as if the angel hears Naamah's thought, and maybe she does. She pulls Naamah's body down by the hips, holds her down at her shoulder with her left hand as she pushes her right fingers in, and she's on the spot before Naamah can let out a breath. When Naamah does breathe, it comes out a scream. Naamah pushes her nails into the angel's back.

She wants to know more about the angel's body, but she can do nothing about that now. She's busy shaking, feeling like she might shit, like she might explode. The angel places her hand on Naamah's stomach, down low, fingers in her hair, and applies pressure to steady her in the water. Naamah wonders if the water shook all the way to the surface. All the way to the boat.

---

THE NEXT DAY, the angel asks, "Does one of the children remind you of yourself? Is that why you come?"

"No. Why would you ask that?"

"It seems like a human thing to do."

"How long have you been watching humans?"

"Since the beginning of humans, who didn't look like humans, and before that. Since the beginning of this world."

"What do you mean, humans did not look like humans?"

"They resembled humans, but if one came up to you, you would not think it a human—perhaps an animal, a cross between a human and an animal. Or someone from another world entirely."

"We grew to be this way? In how we look and talk, you mean?"

The angel nods and looks intently at Naamah.

"Is there something else?"

"God did not kill you all for growing too violent. He said that, but it's not true."

"But we had grown too violent."

"Yes. And you will be violent again."

"Then why?"

"He was jealous. Children of God had begun to indulge themselves with the human women. And more than that, promising themselves to them."

"Can He not do what He wishes with women?"

"He can. He has."

"God does not speak to me," Naamah says.

"I am the presence of God, at least in part. And I speak to you."

"I'm not sure whether I want Him to speak to me."

"He speaks to me constantly."

"Right now? I thought you hadn't been found—didn't want to be found. What does He say?"

"It's not like human speech with me. He wants me to return, and I feel that the way I might feel the sun on me. Or the way you might hear a loud sound in your chest rather than your ears."

"Is He angry with you?"

"Yes."

"Will He kill you if you return?"

"He could kill me here."

"Why hasn't He?"

"There are far fewer angels than humans."

"How many angels are there?"

"There are things even you shouldn't know, Naamah."

"Do you have a family?"

"Not in the way you think of one. But the others are dear to me. He is dear to me."

"Am I dear to you?"

"No," the angel lies.

"Then maybe I will stop coming."

"Soon you will not come, because of the water's decline, and there is nothing you or I can do about that. You will be restored to the world of the living."

# TWELVE

The next day, Naamah's kept from visiting. Sadie asks her to come to the room of horses. She says, "He seems ill. He's pawing at the ground."

When Naamah reaches the room, she sees only a disturbance in the hay on the floor. "I hear him, but tell me what's happening."

"His back is on the ground now, and he's tossing back and forth."

"We'll need everyone. Gather them all on the deck and send Noah down here."

Naamah waits. She hears the horse's legs fall against the floor, and she jumps at the sound of the hooves banging against the side of the stall. She closes her eyes until Noah is there.

"Is he all right?" Noah asks.

"I don't think so."

"What's the plan?"

"I was thinking we push him off the boat onto the patch of land and hope the fall breaks his neck."

Noah looks surprised, but he says, "Okay."

"Unless you want to try to suffocate a horse."

"I don't."

"Then can you tie rope around him and we'll try to get him up to the deck?"

He nods.

No one in the family is happy to hear the plan, but they follow it because all of their strength is needed to get the terrified horse over the railing.

They listen as the horse hits the ground with a bang.

"Is he dead?" Naamah asks.

"Looks like it," Ham says.

"What now?" Adata asks.

"I'll go find out why he was sick. And that will determine what we do next. None of you go too far."

NAAMAH RUNS her hands over the dead horse. She finds the middle point between the two front legs and holds her right hand there while she swoops her left hand over the stomach and up between the two back legs to the anus. This is the path her old bone will take, the one she carries with her, ground to such a sharpness. She fights through the skin, sometimes sliding her right hand in to hold the skin taut.

She slips both hands inside to find the intestines, cut them free, pull them out. Once they begin to slide out, they keep coming. Naamah sits back and listens to them slide over each other and settle onto the ground.

She takes hold, gets both hands around a coil, and then she starts moving her hands along it, careful not to miss any spread of flesh, not sure what she will find.

When she finds it, she feels foolish in her careful patience. There's a place in the intestines that's so firm and full. She runs her bone along it and pushes her thumb through. She feels the dozens of worms there, filling the intestine to obstruction, wriggling and alive.

THE BOYS USED to bathe in the shallows of the river. Naamah made them little toys, hammering holes in the bottoms of old cups. They held them up so that one cup showered into the next, into the next. Or they held them up over one another's heads.

Naamah sat in the shade until they tired themselves. Then she washed each of them. She wondered when they could be trusted to wash themselves, or when it would be safe to allow them to walk to the river themselves.

She often thought of what little things she would be free of when they were grown. She wouldn't worry when they coughed while eating. She wouldn't think of whether they'd had an easy time falling asleep.

She couldn't imagine the new concerns that would replace these, following God's word.

SHE ASKS THEM all to come down and help her push the dead horse into the water. They sweat and grunt and soon he is underwater. They wait until he rises back to the surface, the way dead bodies do, and then they keep pushing him.

"I can't," Neela says. "I can't keep going."

"No, of course, go rest," Naamah says.

The rest of them swim the horse out.

"How much longer?" Ham asks.

"I don't know. I don't want him floating next to the boat, do you?" Naamah says.

They get far enough that no one could argue that they hadn't done their best. Before climbing back to land, Naamah pauses to splash her face with water.

"Naamah!" Sadie says, in a gasp.

"What is it?"

"I'm sorry," she says. "Nothing. It's just, the water doesn't seem as clean now, with the worms, and the dead horse."

Naamah laughs. "I guess it doesn't." She is deciding whether to hold her tongue about how the water is already filled with death.

BACK ON BOARD, they brush the horses one by one, making sure there are no larvae in their hair, manes, tails. They lead each clean horse to the room of milking goats, to the room of sheep, to be with any animals that will tolerate the large horses and not be killed by worms.

Adata gets a dog to help her herd goats into the horses' stalls to eat the remaining hay. While they eat, Adata checks the walls for larvae. She tries to be as meticulous as she can, as Naamah would be if she could see them. She brushes all the remaining hay to one stall of the room, where the goats can gather around it. Then she scours the floor. She finds only two larvae. All that work for two. But maybe the goats have eaten more.

They lead most of the horses back to their stalls. Noah has ended up on the deck with a horse who grew restless.

While Naamah goes to Noah, the others check Adata's work.

"What if they already all have worms?" Sadie asks quietly.

"I don't know," Adata says.

"But then there will be no horses in the new world."

"Maybe God is fine with that."

"He will not punish us for failing one of his creatures?"

"I don't think so," Adata says, but only to comfort Sadie, not out of any firm belief of her own that they are ever far from God's grief.


NOAH IS WATCHING the horse throw its head and stomp the deck in a forceful rhythm.

"She will not settle," Noah tells Naamah.

"Maybe she loved the horse we took away."

"Maybe so," Noah says. "I don't think the sight of the water is helping."

"Can we move her back to a room?"

"I'm worried she'll hurt another animal."

"We can't kill her and feed her to the bigger animals until we know she doesn't have worms. We'd have to inspect her stool, maybe cut her open—"

"That's not what I want," he says. "That's not what I meant."

The horse neighs.

Noah adds, "I'm sure she'll calm."

They're silent.

"Sing to her," Noah says.

"You sing to her," she whips back. "Sorry. I didn't— Just— Why don't you pat her on her side? Like a gallop."

He does, and soon the sound of the horse's clanging hooves disappears. Only the neighing continues, between heavy breaths. Naamah reaches out her hands and walks toward the sound. When she gets close, she stops and looks down at the deck. The horse stretches her head into her waiting hands. Through the horse's head Naamah can feel Noah's steady pounding.

"I'm sorry he got sick," Naamah says. "I've done everything I can so that no more of you get sick. So that you don't get sick. I'll do my best for you."

The horse shakes her head a little.

"Don't worry about all that water. That'll be gone soon. You'll be free soon. I will make sure you are free."

Naamah moves her hands slowly up the horse's head and blocks her eyes from seeing behind and to the side of her.

"Better, right? Just look at me. You are fine. Yes? You are fine."

The horse calms, and Noah leads the horse back down to the stalls.


THE NEXT DAY, Naamah returns to the angel's world.

"Hello," says the angel.

"I'm sorry I wasn't here yesterday. A horse got sick," she says.

"I wonder," the angel says, not caring about the horse, "if you can't see animals, does that mean you can't tell if you pass one in the water, swimming down here? Or if there's one here, beside you now?"

"No, I can't," Naamah says.

"Does that mean you can move through them, do you think? Does one of your senses have the power to bend another to its will?"

"No. I can still feel the animals. I've never swum into something in the water."

"Then it might be accurate to picture giant sea monsters swimming about you in languid circles as you make your way to me?"

"Yes."

"Then I will picture it so."

"Why?"

"I have thought about this. Why this picture of you rises again and again in my mind. I think it must be satisfying for me, to see you in a vulnerable position that you're unaware of."

"Is that not my whole life, circled by God?"

"No, definitely not. You are far too aware of Him."

Naamah laughs, but the angel continues as if she has not heard. "There is no unguarded moment in your life."


THAT NIGHT, when Naamah's back on the boat, she runs to the cold room where she stores the seeds. There are root vegetables stored there, too. She reaches her hand into the sand until she finds a carrot. She pulls it out slowly and pats the sand back down where she's disturbed it, and then she takes the carrot to the horse, as an apology.

## THIRTEEN

When Naamah goes back underwater again, the angel is not there.

"Naamah, will you stay with us?" a child asks.

"For now."

"We are playing a game."

"Ah, what is the game?"

"We are deciding which animal we will be. Are you any good at that game?"

"I am quite good at that game," says Naamah.

"I'm going to be a vulture!" yells one child.

"I'm a camel!"

"I'm a wolf!" And the child howls at the sparkling archway above them.

"What will you be, Naamah?"

"A worm, surely," she says, and she wriggles her hands to their bellies and tickles them.

"No! No!" they yell through laughter. "You can't be a worm."

"You're much too beautiful, Naamah!"

"Too big!"

Naamah laughs. "All right then, I'm an elephant." She hunches over, throws her arm out in front of her face, and trumpets.

The children run around screaming. "She will trample us!"

"Stampede!"

Naamah straightens her back when their joy seems no longer to do with her being an elephant. One child stops near her and holds her hand.

"Are you all right?" she asks him.

The boy nods.

"Do you know where the angel is?"

He shakes his head.

"Does anyone know?"

"Maybe," he says, and he leads her away from the children, out to a small cave that the angel has filled with strings of crystal like endless garland. When they arrive, the child leaves her without going in.

"Hello?" Naamah says as she enters the cave.

"Hello," comes the voice of a woman.

"I'm Naamah."

"I know." She comes out to face Naamah. She's tall and thin and beautiful and young, but also very clearly dead.

"What are you doing here?" Naamah asks.

"You mean, in this cave, or more like, why am I not in the proper world of the dead, since I'm not a confused, lost child?"

Naamah nods. "The second one," she says, realizing she's already come off as rude.

"I like it here. And it's not like that world is some realm independent of Him. I can't imagine knowingly going to Him after what He's done."

"You remember the flood?"

"Vividly," she says. "I am not one of the children. I remember pain. I remember eating and how strong smells can be. I remember my family."

"You had children?"

"You have played with my boy."

Naamah turns back to see if the boy is still in sight, but he's not. "That was him?"

The woman nods. "He doesn't remember me."

"At all?"

"Doesn't seem to. Though I've told him I'm his mother." The woman moves around the cave.

"Do you want him to go to the next world?"

"Yes and no."

"If he does go, will you follow him?"

"Yes." The woman stops. "Why do you keep asking me questions you know the answers to?"

"I'm sorry."

"Well, say what you're here to ask already."

"Do you know where the angel is?"

"I think she is with Him."

"Will she come back?" Naamah asks.

"I think so. Don't you?"

"Yes, I do."

"Come back tomorrow, Naamah."

Naamah nods and starts to leave.

"And bring me something."

Naamah looks back at her. "Like what?"

"Something of the world of the living," she says, excited.


THE NEXT DAY, on the boat, Naamah scours her things. A brush, a candle, food, a seed. Would one of Neela's smuggled paintings not be ruined by the water? A piece of clothing dyed brightly green, perhaps. The thick, layered cloth she uses and reuses for her menstrual blood. A piece of jewelry?

Then she thinks of it. She asks Sadie to help her. They go to a room stacked with wooden boxes, each a home for a group of insects.

"Please, find the golden beetles for me, will you, Sadie? I think they're in this column."

Sadie opens the little doors until she finds them. Naamah sees the morning glories in the box and reaches her hand in, hoping one of the beetles will crawl on.

"Let me help." Sadie reaches in, too, and taps a beetle toward Naamah's hand. When Naamah feels the beetle's hooked feet in her palm, she quickly cups her other hand over it and brings it out. Then she shuts the door and turns to leave.

"Where are you going, Naamah?"

Naamah tries to brush her off, moving quickly down the hall.

"You aren't supposed to take it, Naamah!"

But Naamah keeps going.

————

NAAMAH WADES INTO THE WATER, keeping the beetle above her head until she's nearly under the surface herself, and then she lets her knees give out. She lowers her hands, places the beetle on the back of her arm, shielding it with one hand so it can't float away. It crawls up her arm, alive and well. The beetle can hold its breath by holding an air bubble to its mouth, but that bubble might not be enough for this trip, and she admits to herself that she might be killing the beetle. Accepting the risks, she gathers the beetle back in her hands and dives down.

NAAMAH REACHES THE CAVE and presents the beetle.

"Spectacular!" says the woman. "Look at that. Look at it move!"

"You can keep it," Naamah says.

"Yes? Then I will. For a few days at least." She takes the beetle from Naamah and puts it on her shoulder.

Naamah watches small loops of thread get pulled on the woman's dress.

"She's touched you, hasn't she?" the woman asks. "The angel, I mean."

Naamah's surprised. "Yes," she says.

"I want someone to touch me. I want to know if I can still feel what I remember. Will you touch me?"

Naamah hesitates.

"Please."

Naamah leans over and kisses the woman, opens her mouth to

receive her tongue. But the woman's tongue is covered in water, and for a moment Naamah thinks she might drown kissing her. Naamah gags and then she feels bad that she's gagged. She tries to grab the woman's waist, her hips, but she slides over them. She has to hook her entire arm around her to hold her close, but Naamah is determined to help the woman, to see what her body is and isn't after death. The woman spreads her legs so Naamah can put two fingers in her, four, and while Naamah feels hardly anything, maybe the woman feels more.

"Does it feel good?" Naamah asks.

The woman begins to cry and pushes her away. "I don't think I'm human anymore."

"Couldn't you try with someone down here? Maybe it's only that I'm . . . that I can't help."

"They aren't curious anymore. They don't care about their bodies— the great abandonment of our bodies. That's what I like to call the flood sometimes. The great abandonment. That everyone took part in." She's still crying, but she's angry now, too, looking all around the room and swinging her arms. "Him abandoning us, us abandoning our bodies, a forced abandonment of our children, and our children of us in some cases. Though I guess that's not how you've experienced it." She takes the beetle off her shoulder and places it on the table. She watches the beetle instead of looking at Naamah. It crawls along, with its long pauses, as if full of thought. Without looking up, she asks, "How have you experienced it?"

"I guess I think of it as more of a reclamation."

"But how have *you* experienced it?"

"I have always experienced it as if I were outside of it. Like when you're so tired, and all you want to do is go to bed, but you haven't cleaned up the food, and if you don't clean up the food, ants will come." The woman seems to be calming down as she listens to her, so Naamah keeps going. "In the morning, ants will be everywhere, following their set pathways all over the food. So you start cleaning the food. You start with something small. Very easy to complete. And when you finish it, you remark upon its doneness, so achieved, and you continue to the next thing. And you go on like that until you have cleaned everything, when you thought you could not, and you collapse into bed and go to sleep."

"And in this scenario—what will you do when you get to go to bed?"

"When the land is dry again?" Naamah says. "I don't know. I don't know what sleep looks like in that idea of the world He puts in front of me."

"If I were you, I'd figure that out." The woman looks at her for the first time since they kissed, takes her time looking over Naamah's face, her lips and eyes and hair, and it makes Naamah uncomfortable, how alive she feels in that moment.

Looking back at the beetle, the woman says, "I just want to put it in my mouth! What is that about?" But she's not really looking for Naamah's response to that.

"Is the angel back today?" Naamah asks.

"No," she says.

"Then I'll see you again tomorrow." And Naamah leaves.


FINALLY THE ANGEL RETURNS. When Naamah sees her again, she realizes that she had constructed a more concrete image of the angel in her mind, to remember her by. A certain height, a certain shape to her breasts and hips and hair. Now that she's in front of her again, though, the angel is as she was: formless and of too many forms at once. Naamah wants to touch her again. That's when the angel feels real. That's when Naamah feels the most sure of anything.

"Were you with Him?" Naamah asks.

"Yes."

"Does He care about us?"

"I didn't—"

"No, not us. I mean, my family, humans, the boat. Is He paying attention? Is He watching?"

"He is and He isn't."

"What does that mean? Why am I doing what I'm doing?"

"You make your own decisions."

"Never mind." Naamah shakes her head. "I'm surprised you came back."

"Why?"

"I imagine His presence is hard to deny. Just His voice alone made Noah follow Him."

"That had to do with you, too."

"What do you mean?"

"Noah followed His word, but it was to save you and your children."

"When Noah speaks of it, it's not like that."

"It wasn't constant," the angel says.

"No."

"But it was there. Noah would not have completed the ark if it weren't for you."

"You know?"

"I know."

"You make me sound very powerful."

"Yes."

"Well, I am weak. You understand that, right?"

"Yes, weak and powerful both."

"And you? Aren't you exclusively powerful?"

With a smile the angel says, "But I have always known that I am the less interesting of the two of us."

Naamah shakes her head again.

Then the angel says, "Let me ask you something. Am I interesting on my own, or only because of my relationship to Him?"

"You are interesting."

"Answer me again tomorrow."

"I know—"

"No, tomorrow," the angel says.


THAT NIGHT, WHEN NAAMAH LOOKS over the water, Japheth joins her. Naamah finds herself thinking that the mountaintops are reaching higher into the sky now than when she last bothered to consider them, even though she knows it's only the water exhaling, lowering its burdensome chest a little more, like a man returning to normal after he's exerted himself. She looks at Japheth's chest.

"What is it?" he asks.

"Can you imagine the mountains as they were?"

"Yes."

"Now, imagine you met a bird, who said she'd been talking to the mountain. Been inside the mountain, even."

"Okay."

"You'd think that bird was special?"

"Of course."

"Is the bird special only because of its relationship to the mountain?"

"That's why it's especially compelling, I'd say."

"Yes," Naamah says. "So what could make the bird special, would you say, outside of that?"

"Maybe its plumage. Maybe if it could speak, or do something else birds can't usually do."

"Let's say all of that is true, but it's all because of the mountain that the bird can do these things, and that it looks the way it does."

"So the bird talks?"

"Yes."

"Then you'd have to ask the bird to define herself."

"You don't think someone who's grown very close to the bird could answer?"

"Maybe."

"Isn't it more difficult to know yourself anyway?" asks Naamah.

"Do you think you know me better than I know myself?"

Naamah laughs. "Definitely not."

He smiles at her. "Have you met a bird?"

"I think so," she says. And the mountaintops look dangerous under the moon.

———

THE NEXT TIME Naamah dives down, the angel is waiting for her.

Naamah starts, "You are interesting because of Him. You are interesting because you have left Him. I don't know how you are interesting outside of Him, except that you like to imagine things like sea monsters, and you have compassion, and probably there's more." She pauses. "You tell me."

"I don't know."

"Yes, you do."

The angel stops to think and eventually says, "I love the planets made of gas."

"I didn't know there were planets made of gas," Naamah says.

"Yes. One of them is nearly all hydrogen. I can pass through it and its watery depths. Not water. Just watery. And then it gets so dense and heavy the closer to the center you go. I can't make it to the center in this form. And it's hot from all that pressure. And that's why, so far from the sun, it remains gas, does not freeze. It makes dusty rings over its surface, the winds and storms, which—if you must compare one thing to another, over and over to understand it—take the shape of mountains, waves, moles, eyes."

"Keep going," Naamah says.

"That planet has moons, too, more than a dozen, and smaller bodies, too. Celestial bodies. And the storms are formed by the gases, the planet's gravity, the sun's pull, but then the moons get involved, each with their own gravitational forces. One changing the other changing the other. Until who's to say what forms what. Who's to say which bears more weight in forming the identity of the thing."

Naamah kisses her, and they have sex.

And the next day, they have sex.

And the next day, they have sex.

And the next day, they have sex.

And the next day, they have sex.

And the next day, they have sex.

And the next day, they have sex, and when the angel is above Naamah, kissing her on the mouth, her hands searching Naamah's body, the angel flashes into something else. A tiger.

Naamah pushes her away. "What was that?" she asks.

"What?"

"You were a tiger."

"No, I wasn't."

Naamah turns away from her. "You were a tiger."

"I wasn't."

"Are you an animal?"

"No, wha—"

"Tell me the truth." Naamah's shaking now.

"I am telling you the truth!"

"He sent you?"

"No—"

"What is happening? Have I even left the boat?" Naamah thrashes about in the water, moves her legs like she's marching on the deck, on land, anywhere with air.

The angel grabs her swinging arms. "Stop."

Still facing away from her, Naamah screams, "You're not even real!"

With that, the film around Naamah's body breaks, the water

pours into her mouth, her ears pop, her skin hurts. She kicks as hard as she can to the surface, and when she breaks through she takes in the cold air in gulps.

DURING THE STORM that brought the flood, the tigers made a long, deep, bellowing growl that could have been heard from far away, but there Naamah was on top of it. All through the day, all through the night, under all the noises of the other animals, she heard the tigers.

She wanted them to finish, to roar, to build and deliver a deafening chorus, awful and fearsome. Something to reach God's ear. But only so that on the other side of that roaring, they might be quiet.

The noise moved the air around her into a state of unrest, and that had a warmth to it. She lay in bed and remembered silence. She thought maybe there'd been a tactile component to it that she hadn't realized at the time, maybe silence could produce a chill. She buried herself in blankets until she was sweaty.

When the rains were over, it took Naamah a week to relearn how to sleep through the night without that constant sound; she'd pushed all the other noises into the steadiness of that rain. It reminded her of when the boys were babbling, crawling, and she'd let herself pay attention to something else, anything else, until she was startled by an instant of silence. Because that meant they'd found something worth finding. That meant they'd brought it to their mouths.

## FOURTEEN

The next morning, Naamah wonders if her ability to be underwater is gone for good, but she's not ready to know. She stays on the boat all day. And while she knows that she's hurt the angel, she's still filled with doubt. The tiger was so real to her, right in front of her face, real enough that she doesn't trust God anymore. The longer she is on the boat, the less she trusts Him, and His feelings toward her, and His choice of her for matriarch. Figurehead.

IN A HALLWAY on the second floor, Sadie corners her.

"Naamah," she starts. "I counted the beetles." But she loses her confidence quickly.

Naamah touches her arm. "I will bring it back," she says.

"Really?"

"Yes."

"It's not dead?"

"It's not dead," Naamah says. But she's not sure that's true.

———————

NAAMAH TUCKS A MORNING GLORY into her dress before she heads down the ladder to the water. They leave the ladder set up all the time now. Naamah sometimes catches herself worrying that someone will sneak onto the boat, and then she remembers there is no one.

SHE KEEPS HER HEAD above water, treading, for a long time—but eventually she has to find out. She puts her head under, closes her eyes, and presses her tongue forward. The thin film is there. She wants to see this as the angel's forgiveness, but as she gets closer to the village, as she swims through it, the angel is nowhere to be seen. Naamah heads for the cave.

Inside, the woman is carving into the wall.

"Hello? Hello!" Naamah repeats, louder and louder over the woman's hammering, trying not to surprise her.

"Naamah! Hello!"

"Is the beetle still here?"

"How are you? What are you working on?"

"What?"

"Oh, the things you might say to me if you were interested in seeing me." She smiles and crosses her arms, long and thin like the rest of her. "You know, if you weren't just here for the beetle."

"Right, yes, I'm sorry."

She shakes her hand. "Teasing. Teasing."

"I just wanted to get back."

"It's okay." She puts down her tools. "The beetle has been hanging out on that table."

Naamah swims over and looks to the woman, who dips her hand and points up, underneath the table. Naamah ducks down to look. The beetle is there, walking slowly, but Naamah can't see it.

"Will you get it for me and put it on top of the table? On top of this?" She takes the morning glory out of her pocket.

The woman lifts the beetle with a finger and puts it on the morning glory. Naamah sees a spot of pressure on a petal. She leans down and blows to make a bubble—by instinct, not sure it will work—and out it comes, a perfect sphere around the morning glory.

"What are you working on?" Naamah asks.

The woman looks up at the patterns she's been making in the rock. "I'm not sure yet. You like it?"

"Yes." Naamah looks at the tools. "Are you good with those?"

The woman laughs, rolling her eyes, as if to say, *Look at these walls.*

"I mean," Naamah tries again, "would you be good enough, with your tools, to do that on a tooth?"

"Oh," the woman says. "I think so."

"I want something, on a back molar, on top. I want to remember."

"What do you want?"

"Two lines, next to each other."

"Right now?"

"Yes."

"Okay," she says. "You know this might make you more likely to lose the tooth one day?"

"Then pick a tooth I won't mind losing," Naamah says.

Inside her mouth, the dead woman's hands drip with floodwater as she works.

WHEN SHE'S FINISHED, Naamah scoops up the bubble with the beetle on its half-eaten morning glory. The woman asks, "Will the beetle be all right?"

"Yes."

"I heard about the horse."

"You did?" Naamah's surprised.

"The angel told me."

"I didn't know she saw that."

"She saw you put your fingers through the worms as they spilled out of the sliced intestine."

Naamah nods, with her head at an angle—not to say yes, just to mark the thought.

"You really can't see them?"

"Not right now."

"Why do you think the beetle will survive?" the woman asks.

"Because He wants it to."

"Didn't He want the horse to survive?"

"I thought so," Naamah says.

"Then you can't really say about the beetle, can you?"

"I know that, back in its box, you wouldn't be able to tell this one from the others."

"That's not fair."

"Horses die of worms. I can't prevent that."

"He could prevent it," says the woman.

"He could."

"I want the beetle to live."

"You probably want all the animals to live. Come stay on the boat with me and see how you feel about them then."

"You don't want them to?"

"I think them living is as much up to them as it is to me."

"I do want them all to live," the woman says softly.

"I know."

"I thought that I didn't want anything He wants."

"And here you are, distraught over a beetle." Naamah laughs, and the woman nods. "The beetle can stop, like a hibernating bear. It can take care of itself."

"Thank you," she says.

"Thank you for my tooth." Naamah runs her tongue over it and feels the two lines, not too sharp.

"If you come back to the cave, Naamah, come back to see me. Not to ask about the angel. And if you don't want to see me, that's fine. I don't want anything else from you. I worry that I haven't made my-self clear. Do you know what I mean?"

"I do."

"Okay. Then I'm getting back to work."

Naamah swims off with the beetle as the woman hammers away behind her.


THE ANGEL REACHES HER BEFORE she's back to the shallow water near the boat.

"I'm sorry I left you like that, so deep underwater," she says.

"I made it, didn't I?"

"Yes, I was pleased to see that."

"I'm sorry I said you're not real."

"Yes. I am real."

"I know."

"I am not a tiger."

Naamah doesn't respond to this.

"I'm not planted here by Him to keep an eye on you, or to keep you happy or distracted."

"I'm sorry."

"I don't want you to be sorry; I want you to believe me."

"I don't know how to believe you when I don't understand Him."

"He doesn't care as much about you as you think, Naamah."

"No, He's just given me responsibility for everything He does care about."

"No. I—" The angel pauses. "I meant for that to come out as a good thing. That you might relax at the thought of Him."

"He killed everyone! Everyone! How can I relax at the thought of Him?"

"Naamah, please."

"I don't know Him and I don't want to know Him."

"Naamah, you're crushing the beetle."

Naamah releases her grip. "Shit." She calms down. "Is it okay?"

"It is," the angel says.

"I have to go."

The angel leaves first, and Naamah can't help looking for a hint of a tiger's gait as she moves through the water.

———

"Sadie!" Naamah yells, back on the boat, below deck.

Sadie pops out of a doorway.

Naamah takes her hand and puts the beetle into it. "See? It's fine."

"Thank you."

"Will you put it away for me?"

"Yes," she says, and suddenly she tears up.

"Sadie—"

"It's nothing. Nothing. Every time I open a door, I expect to see more dead animals, or sick animals, or missing animals. And you whisk one away and return it like it's nothing. You get the dam to accept the lamb again. How, Naamah?"

"It's not like that. I haven't done anything."

"I know. I know. But how are you not defeated by all of this?"

"I can't even see them, Sadie. I want to love them and fear them, and I can't even see them."

But Sadie's hardly listening to Naamah now. "It's our job not to fail, and yet I feel surrounded by possible failures. I lie in bed at night thinking of ways we might fail."

"Your only job is to live. It's my job to take care of the animals. I'm so grateful for all the help you give, but don't think, as you clean the rooms, feed the animals, that any of them are more important than you." She lifts Sadie's chin. "You can worry only about yourself, okay?"

"Naamah?"

"Yes."

"What if I don't want to have children when we get off the boat?"

Naamah takes her time. She knows Sadie well enough to know there will come a point in her life when she's so flooded with the desire for a child that she will feel it inside her body like a hunger. Not a painful one, not like when you're actually hungry, but when you're full and thinking ahead to the next thing you'll eat, if you could choose anything in the world. How Naamah often feels now, on the boat, about a piece of fresh fruit, an orange maybe. Everything in your body says it will be right, it will be perfect.

"See how you feel after Neela has her child. There's no rush. What a wonderful aunt you will make."

Sadie's quiet.

"Aren't you excited to be an aunt?"

"I am." And she's sincere in that.

Naamah wonders if God has considered this: women so distrustful of Him that they might never bear children for the new world.

UNDER THE WATER AGAIN, Naamah's with the children, playing with blocks the angel made them. Naamah haphazardly makes a tower with the walls in the shape of a heart. "Look," she tells the children. They come over and stare down the middle of it.

"That looks like a pretty damaged heart," says one of the children.

Naamah laughs.

Another child reaches his hand in, says, "It's acidy in here!"

Naamah laughs again. "That's your stomach," she says. "Blood is almost like water."

"Water!"

"Yes."

"Really water?"

"Yes," Naamah says. And she thinks, *Not so different from how you are now.*

ANOTHER DAY, Naamah returns and finds one girl playing alone.

"Hi, Naamah!"

"Hello."

"Would you like to play with me?"

"I would. That's why I came."

The girl smiles and shows Naamah a game where they clap their hands and then slap them with each other, first the backs of their hands, then the front, and after the next clap, they must do it twice, back-front, back-front, and so on, and so on, as far along as they can get without messing up. They make it to six. The girl is a mess of giggles. She falls forward into Naamah's chest.

When she sits back up, she looks as if she wants to speak, but she lifts up her clothing first. "My chest looks the same as every other child's, Naamah. It's flat, smooth, bony, brown. And my nipples are as small as my fingertips."

"Yes."

She lowers her clothing again. "The women here, the men—every chest is different. Each woman's breasts are a different size, some covered in stretch marks, some with larger nipples than others, some that stick out all the time. The men are wider and slighter, hairy and not, sagging and not."

"Yes."

"I like how different everyone looks. If all the children held their clothes over their heads, I don't think you'd know which one I was, would you?"

"I don't know."

"You wouldn't. I don't think so," the girl says. "Will I grow breasts?"

Naamah holds back tears. "No, darling."

The girl doesn't say anything.

"Are you okay?" Naamah asks.

"I'm dead."

"You—"

"I heard the angel say it."

Naamah reaches out and takes the girl's hands.

"It makes sense. And you aren't dead?"

"No."

"Do you want to be dead?"

Naamah shakes her head.

"Is it bad to be dead?"

"No!" She pulls the girl in and holds her. "No, of course it's not. It's just another way to be."

"A way that doesn't grow."

"Not your body."

The girl pulls away from Naamah. "There are things I'll miss out on, never being a woman."

"A few things."

"Like I'll never have a child."

"Yes."

"I'll never have sex."

"Yes."

"You and the angel have sex."

Naamah nods slowly.

"I've seen you."

Naamah tenses a little.

"It's okay." The girl rubs Naamah's arm, how a child would, her hand flat and light on Naamah's skin. Not quite a comfort, but a gesture of comfort. "If you've already had sex, and you have children, why then? Why not die?"

"I want to sometimes."

"I think you should," says the girl.

"I will, but for now I want to stay with my children. I want to meet my grandchildren."

"Will you tell them about me?"

"If you want me to."

The girl nods quickly.

"I don't know your name."

The girl stops nodding. "I don't remember it."

Naamah doesn't know what to say.

"Tell them you met a girl who could never grow up," the girl says, pulling back to look into Naamah's eyes, "but she imagined that if she did grow up, she would be tall and fat, with giant breasts and giant nipples, and stretch marks everywhere, and she would have a dozen children, and they would all eat cream on everything and run around laughing, and they would paint her body with their hands, hundreds of purple stains and smears, until she looked like, like—"

"Like a god." But Naamah regrets it as soon as she says it.

"Yes, like a god," the dead girl says.

———

Naamah starts the next day milking a cow. It's easy enough to find her way to a cow and its teat. Milking always reminds her of when she was breastfeeding, how she could press her own breast back at the nipple's edge, follow that with a squeeze, down toward the tip, flatly on each side, flat like a wedge, and the milk would come out of at least four different places, sometimes straight up in the air. She remembers how she laughed at that, and how the baby was small and didn't laugh at anything.

She runs the cow's milk through a clean cloth and takes it up to her family.


On a day like any other, Naamah wakes thinking of Bethel and can't get out of bed. She tells Noah she's tired. He brings her snacks throughout the day as he thinks to. A bowl of grain. Then raisins. In the evening, he brings her peeled and sliced jicama.

"You went into the room for this," she says.

"I did."

"You shouldn't have."

"The water is going down fast enough, I think. I can spoil you tonight."

She takes a slice and bites it.

"Are you feeling better?"

She nods, chewing.

"Do you want to talk about it?"

She shakes her head. "I want to lie here and eat jicama slices in the dark."

He smiles. "So be it!" He leaves the room and closes the door without even a creak.

WHEN SHE WAKES THE NEXT DAY, she throws her legs over the side of the bed, forcing herself up so quickly that she blacks out, and she has to rest her forehead on the wall until her vision comes back. Up on the deck, at breakfast, Neela still tosses bread to the animals when she thinks Naamah won't notice. Naamah wants so badly to see an animal she almost can't stand it. She decides to go back to the cave, where there are no animals to see. She doesn't even wait until the end of breakfast to go down the ladder.

At the cave, the woman has covered one wall completely. The angel has inset lighted crystals into all the paths the woman has chipped away.

"Do you like it?" she asks. "I asked the angel to do it for me."

"It's stunning," Naamah says, looking at the wall and thinking of how the angel must spend time here, with this woman, when Naamah's not around.

"Thank you."

"What's the pattern?"

"What does it look like to you?" she asks.

Naamah answers, "It looks like something growing."

The woman looks at it, too.

"Is it?"

The woman smiles. "No."

"Well, what then?"

"Does it matter?"

"Yes," Naamah says, "I want to know."

"My husband used to trace shapes on my back. I don't know what they were, but it felt so good. He could do it for almost an hour without tiring. We would lie down and he would watch the sunset and trace those shapes, and I would say I was watching the sunset, too, but my eyes were closed." She gestures toward the wall. "I was trying to remember. I don't know if I did."

Naamah watches her face and can tell it doesn't matter if the woman got it right—it's filling her with joy.

The woman goes up to the wall and runs her hand over the strings of crystals. Naamah watches the light shine on her hand, then between her fingers, on her face, on her eyes, which already looked covered in oil.

## FIFTEEN

The next time Naamah goes down to the water, the angel stops her.

"You've been avoiding me," the angel says.

"Yes."

"You still think I am a tiger."

Naamah shakes her head.

"You do. I know it. Doesn't it sound foolish to you?"

"Of course it does," Naamah says.

"But that doesn't mean you don't believe it."

"You keep telling me that I don't understand Him. You say you're a part of Him. I am done making assumptions. Isn't that what you want?"

"Not if it means you don't trust me anymore," the angel says.

"I don't know what you want," Naamah says.

"I trust you even though I don't understand you."

"It's different. You know I'm not capable of anything extraordinary."

The angel swims back and forth, furious to be misunderstood. And then she stops. "Do you want to see me as a tiger?"

Naamah knows that if she trusted the angel, if she loved her, now would be the moment to say no.

"Do you?"

"Yes!" Naamah admits. "Yes."

The angel can't hide that she's upset. "Fine." She shakes her whole body, breaks free of her form, and takes the form of a tiger. But it's not the tiger Naamah saw. The angel has the appearance of fur, but without the countless individual hairs that make up the coat of a tiger. And the color isn't right. She is not any individual tiger.

She swims through the water, she paces, she roars.

"I get it," Naamah says.

"What?" the angel says, her woman's voice still inside the tiger's body.

"I get it!" Naamah's upset now, too.

The angel comes back to her woman form. "You shouldn't be upset. You got what you wanted."

"But then what did I see before?"

"I don't know, Naamah. But it wasn't me."

"I'm sorry."

"You shouldn't come down here anymore."

"But—"

"I don't want you here. This place is not for you. The children are spoiled by you."

"Okay."

"You know it's up to me if you breathe down here or not. That you don't drown."

"I know."

"You can get back to the boat, but that's it. Don't try to come again."

"Can I say goodbye to the children?"

"No." The angel moves in front of her as if she might physically stop her. "Don't make me change my mind about your breath." She looks as if she might fight Naamah to the ground.


BACK ON THE PATCH OF LAND, Naamah can't stop sobbing. Her sides hurt. Her breath wheezes. Noah hears her from the deck and rushes down the ladder.

"Are you all right?"

Naamah lets him hold her.

"What happened?"

"I betrayed someone," she gets out.

"Who?"

She looks at him, and he watches on her face as her sadness is overwhelmed by fear. "God," she says. "I think I might have betrayed God."

"No."

"No?" Naamah asks.

"We would know, wouldn't we? He would make it known."

"When did you last hear from Him?"

"Before the rains."

Naamah pulls away from him. "He hasn't spoken to you since before the rains?"

"No."

"Why wouldn't He speak to you?"

"We're still working on the first task He gave us, aren't we?"

"You're not concerned?"

"No," Noah says. "And you shouldn't be, Naamah. I'm here. We've done everything asked of us. You've done everything, taking care of us. All of us."

"I think He might punish me. He might already be punishing me," Naamah says, but she's gone cold to it again, knowing she will keep moving forward regardless.

NAAMAH WALKS THE DARK HALLS of the boat. She hears the animals and pretends she'd be able to see them if she opened the doors. She takes her steps slowly, remembers their shit, their food, the births of their young, their deaths, their patterned stripes and spots, their fur and wool and feathers. She is so full of the details of their invisible bodies.

To keep from clenching her jaw, she runs her tongue over her teeth—over the outside of her bottom teeth, right to left, over the inside, left to right. She remembers discovering a chip once, on an upper molar, extra sharp, a place for her tongue to catch, like clothing on splintered wood. But it's been worn down over the years. Almost every tooth has a dullness to it.

She still loves the lines she asked the dead woman to make.

Then she hears the voice again. "Jael, Jael." One of the cockatoos. "Jael, Jael."

She opens the door. She thinks she can feel all the animals' eyes on her. And then one of them crashes into her chest. She falls back against the wall. She's about to swat it down as hard as she can, maybe kill it, with the great force of her arms, when she realizes that the cockatoo isn't attacking her, just digging his talons into her shirt, steadying himself on her chest. She holds him there, runs her hands over his head and down his back.

"Jael," he says. "Jael."

"Hello, Jael," she says.

"Hello," he says. But it's only a greeting. His nibbling on her finger is what feels affectionate.

They stay like that for a long time, but eventually Naamah has to leave.

THAT DAY IS followed by another day when Naamah cannot leave her bed.

"What is it?" Noah asks.

"I'm tired. We've been on the boat for more than eight months. Aren't you tired?"

"I've been sleeping well," he jokes.

Naamah whacks him on the arm.

"I don't know what to tell you, Naamah. I like it here. I have my family. Tending to the animals fills my days. I'm happy."

"I love that about you." She takes his hand and smiles at him for a moment. "But I'm tired of it."

"Maybe it's all right to be tired of it. Maybe we're supposed to get tired of it. Maybe I'll be tired of it next week. You can bring me things in bed."

"I would."

"You better."

"Okay, but today I'm staying in bed. I'm going back to sleep even."

He leans down and kisses her.

But she doesn't go to sleep right away. She lies there with her eyes closed.

In the desert, Naamah used to envision violent scenarios in her head. What would she do if a man stopped her on the way home from the market? If a man came into her home? In one scenario, she imagined herself dropping to the ground, wrapping her arms around his calves, and throwing her weight into him until he toppled forward over her back. She saw herself swiveling around, over him, putting her knee into the center of his back. She'd grab his hair and lift his head, slice his neck with her sharpened bone.

Even with almost every human on the planet dead, playing out these visions has been a hard habit for her to break. It calms her, makes her feel in control—if not in control of the world, then in control of her body.

After she kills another dangerous man in her head, she opens her eyes. She lights a candle and holds her hand up to the light. She sees the hundreds of lines, the thousands of swirls, over every inch of it, as if the skin has been cobbled together over an arrangement of bones that was never meant to be.

She drops her hand, lifts her wrist, and lets the light run down her forearm. There isn't one swirl. There's a slip of a muscle underneath, moving diagonally toward the elbow. There's one vein lying over one tendon near the wrist. Smooth and perfect, and shadowed by the candle's light. She wonders why her body was meant to be like this and keeps wondering until she falls asleep.

# Naamah

------

When Naamah opens her eyes again, Adata is standing in the doorway.

"Have you given up?" Adata asks.

Naamah's still waking. "What? Given up what?"

"Have you given up on *us*? The ark? Everything?"

"No! Why would you think that?"

"You've spent two days of the last week in bed. You're the one who's always plowing ahead, unfazed by dead animals, broken doors, injured legs, the same food over and over."

"Adata, did you come down here just to give me shit?"

"Yes."

"Why?"

"Because," Adata yells, "when you give up, they do! Shem doesn't make jokes, Ham's not an ass. Sadie looks like she might break, and Neela doesn't know if it's better to hold her or let her go ahead and do it already."

"But Noah's strong."

"He helps you, but the rest of them—they follow your lead."

Naamah shakes her head. "I don't want them to."

"Tough." Adata stares at her, and her steadiness steadies Naamah. "Now get out of bed."


Naamah meets them all for dinner up on the deck, and Adata was right—everyone is quiet.

"I'm sorry I haven't been around," Naamah says.

"It's fine, Mom," Japheth says.

"I'll be around more now. I promise."

Adata gives her a look, urging her on.

"And I'm excited for what comes next." She forces a smile.

"Here, here!" says Noah.

"Tomorrow we should make a stew with the vegetables we've been saving," Naamah says, trying to lift her voice.

"Because you think the water will be down soon?" Sadie asks.

"I do."

"I will make it," Adata says.

"Great. Thank you," Naamah says.

"I want to help with the stew, too," Neela says. She kisses Ham. Everyone's mood is beginning to lighten. All it takes is Naamah saying each sentence with a grin.

The sunset shines behind all of them, breaking the sky into pinks and oranges, letting the pale blue give way to the deep blue, showing that one color cannot just lighten or darken to another; it must forget itself completely before it finds itself again.


NAAMAH HELPS Adata and Neela find the vegetables in the sand and choose which to take, and how many. They start to prepare the meal on the deck so that the scent of it might not grow too strong among the animals.

Naamah makes an excuse to go down the ladder. She undresses on the patch of land, leaves her clothes over a ladder's rung. She has to see. She has to know. *Is the angel done with me?*

Under the water, the feeling is unfamiliar at first: the held breath, the pressure creating air bubbles in her nose and ears. She feels one little sphere escape her nose, cling for a moment to the edge of her nostril. Then it lets go, rising to the surface. She feels all of it, even the straight line of the bubble, from her body back to the surface.

THE STEW IS DELICIOUS, and everyone praises Adata and Neela for their cooking. Noah stands and says, "It might be time to send out a bird."

"What bird?" Shem asks.

"We could start with a raven."

"This is so exciting!" Neela says.

Naamah knows why they might start with a raven. Noah is still thinking about where all the bodies have gone. If they're floating somewhere, caught somewhere, humans and animals, drowned and bloated, then the raven will find them. Naamah wonders what will happen to her children if they come upon fields of dead.

Adata nudges her. "Aren't you excited?"

"Yes." Naamah smiles. "I think we have many amazing days ahead of us."

"Oh!" Neela says, and she grabs Naamah's hand and places it on her stomach. "Can you feel it?"

Naamah nods. "Strong baby."

Neela blushes with pride.

"Has everyone felt it?" Naamah asks.

"Yes, over this past week."

"I will feel it again!" Sadie says, and she jumps up and rushes over to feel the baby's kicks. Naamah can see that Sadie has nothing to worry about. She'll be a mother soon enough. Adata too. Naamah can see her whole family growing, growing, until she is the mother of nations. For a second she feels the power of a queen, an empress.

But then she is back on a boat eating stew, where she catches a grain of sand on her tooth. She hears it so loud in her bite that it seems for a moment like lightning striking the boat, setting it on fire, as if it might kill them all and foil God's plan, but she keeps chewing, knowing she's being watched, and as the grain finds its way between her teeth again and again and the sound grows familiar, the feeling becomes smaller, more manageable, easy to tuck inside herself, the sound of a flaw, for her to enjoy alone, until she catches the grain in a spot where she can move it back and forth with her jaw, where she can determine its shape and crush it more precisely, into something that can't make a sound.

## SIXTEEN

Naamah's dreaming of a cactus blooming, her feet in the sand, when Sarai comes to her.

"I think I should take you somewhere," Sarai says.

"Then take me."

Naamah feels the sand change underfoot, until it feels like little twisted fibers. She raises a foot as if it could hurt her.

"What is this?"

"It's called carpeting. We're in the house of a young family. There's a mother here, home, with two children under five. They're playing out back."

"Why 'under five'? What does that indicate?" Naamah asks, still investigating the carpet. She digs her toes in, spreads them apart.

"Five years old. When children turn five, they can go to school for free, sit with teachers, learn to read and write."

"And before five?"

"Their parents can pay for a thing called preschool, or for a nanny, or they can stay home themselves. In this family, the mother stays home."

"What about family? What about the other mothers?"

"Look outside," Sarai says, pointing to the window where the light is coming in and inching across the floor.

As Naamah's eye goes to the window, the rest of the room distracts her. The floor is covered in shiny, colorful toys. There are soft animal toys on a sofa. The wall behind the sofa is covered in images of the same two children. There's a fan on the ceiling. She can't name anything she's seeing, but she takes it in.

She walks to the window. It looks like twelve panes of glass, six on top of six. She runs her fingers over them and there's no break in the glass. She looks closer. The window is made of two plates of glass and, between them, something shiny and white, in the shape of four crosses.

"It's for aesthetics," Sarai says. "Mimicking how older windows looked."

All Naamah can muster is, "Oh."

"Look outside," Sarai says again.

Naamah looks through the window to the lush lawn of zoysia grass, a walk lined with marigolds, a trimmed Japanese maple circled by mulch and edged with decorative bricks. Up and down the street are other houses, all similar in shape, all of them with walks and yards and landscaping.

Sarai explains: "The farther the houses are apart, the more desirable the community, the more expensive it seems."

"Isn't everyone lonely?" Naamah asks, her eyes on a decorative statue of a turtle.

"Yes."

"Why live like this?"

"Not everyone does."

"But a lot," Naamah says.

Sarai nods. She's walking around the room, taking the edge of a curtain between her fingers and then letting it slide away.

"Do you spend a lot of time here?" Naamah asks.

"Yes," she says, sitting down on the floor near the toys. "Come here."

Naamah sits across from her and she feels the rug through her clothes.

"Look." Sarai takes a toy of a zebra and walks it up the ramp into a wooden boat.

"Is that what I think it is?"

"Yes. The ark."

Naamah places her hand over the roof, sees how easily it fits in her hand. Noticing how light it is, she lifts the boat off the ground. "Look how cute it is."

"It is."

"Where am I?"

"You're not in this set."

"This set?"

"There are lots of 'Noah's Ark' toy sets. You're in some of them."

"And children play with this?"

"Yes," Sarai says.

"Do they know what happened?"

"They know a story."

"A story without danger or injury, without cleaning up shit day in and day out. Without even heaviness or height!" she says, putting down the boat.

"Just a story. To teach them about a good, God-fearing man."

"Not about God's wrath? Or His compassion?"

"No."

"No, just about Noah." She picks up the Noah figurine. "Why does he look like this?"

"He's old. Bald, hair turned white, beard untrimmed."

Naamah laughs.

"This whole world can be traced back to you," Sarai says.

"Don't say it like that."

"Like what?"

She looks around her. "Like I'm responsible for any of these choices."

"Not responsible, no. But don't you think you made it possible?"

"No," Naamah says, "I don't."

Sarai runs her thumb down the back of a wooden elephant. She asks, "Would you like to see what an old woman looks like?"

"Sure," Naamah says, and she follows Sarai out the door, closes it behind them, pulling the slick gold knob, which looks like it should be cold to the touch and not so plain as it is.

They walk to a park and sit on a bench across from a very old woman.

"Can she see us?" Naamah asks.

"No," Sarai says. "She can't hear us either."

"She doesn't look well."

"She's actually quite healthy for her age."

"Can she lift anything?"

Even Sarai laughs at this. "She can lift what she needs to."

"Will I look like that one day?"

"No."

"Her skin is sort of incredible," Naamah says.

"I know."

The old woman gets up to go home.

"Can we follow her?" Naamah asks.

"Yes."

They follow her back to her house, an apartment building. They take an elevator up. The woman goes into her kitchen and puts some bread in the toaster. If Naamah has wondered if she was dreaming, she doesn't now. How could this be anything but a dream?

Naamah finds the bedroom and lies on the bed, sinks into it a little.

"This is excessive," she says.

Sarai lets out the smallest snort. "You'd get used to it, I think."

Naamah lifts herself up on her elbows. "Can I ask you something?"

"Yes."

"What happens to a woman as beautiful as you are?"

"You mean, what did happen to me?"

"Yes."

"My husband, Abraham, knew how beautiful I was. Everyone knew. And he knew, too, that husbands are killed to get to their wives. So everywhere we went, he presented himself as my brother. I was taken from him and raped, sometimes once, sometimes for weeks, and then I was returned to him. He thought, every time, that I was so happy to see him, to be reunited. That I was grateful for his good planning, that he was, in fact, not dead." Sarai shakes a little. "And maybe I was, the first time. And that's how I knew how to behave the times that followed."

"I'm sorry."

"Me too."

"But that is all before what happened to your son."

"Yes, somehow, after all of that, I settled back into my life with Abraham and we were happy and prosperous and I had my son. And if I don't regret having him, if I love him more than anything in the world, then how can I regret the events that allowed him to come to be?"

"I would."

"No, you wouldn't. Not regret. Spurn maybe. Blame. Wish there had been another way to reach him that did not require a thousand injuries. But if that way does not exist, then regret doesn't feel like an option."

Suddenly there are voices coming from the other room, and Naamah goes to see. The old woman is eating toast with tuna fish in front of a big glass screen.

"Oh," Naamah says again.

"It's a television. People in other cities record shows, like plays, and then send them to people's televisions."

"All around the world people are watching this?"

"Well, this country at least."

"How many people are alive right now?"

"Seven and a half billion people."

"What's a billion?" Naamah asks.

"It goes tens, hundreds, thousands, ten thousands, hundred thousands, millions, ten millions, hundred millions, billions."

"Say it again."

"Tens, hundreds, thousands, ten thousands, hundred thousands, millions, ten millions, hundred millions, billions. So the number before one billion is nine hundred ninety-nine million, nine hundred ninety-nine thousand, nine hundred ninety-nine. It might be easier if I write it out."

"No, I got it. At least I think so. Seven and a half billion." She whistles. "Seven billion five hundred million people?"

"That's right."

"Are they violent?"

"Yes."

"Sinful?"

"Yes."

"But they are spared?"

"They are," Sarai says.

"Do you know why?"

"The covenant."

"What's the covenant?"

"After the flood, it's a promise God makes to Noah."

"To what? Spare violent people?"

"No, to not kill you all ever again."

Naamah doesn't know what to say. Her attention falls on the television again. "What is this show?"

Sarai bends her head around to see. "It's called *Law & Order: SVU*. It's about people figuring out who committed a crime. There are a lot of different versions of the show. This one focuses on crimes against children, sex crimes against women."

"Can we stay? Can I watch?"

Sarai waves her over to the TV.

On the show, one of the detectives is interviewing a priest who might know something about the crime. The priest keeps derailing the conversation to talk about the detective's relationship to his faith. He keeps talking about God's love and forgiveness.

"That's how they talk about God in this time?" Naamah asks.

"Yes," Sarai says.

"When are we?"

"About ten thousand years in the future."

"And this is what God is known for?" Naamah asks.

"Yes."

"Does He speak to anyone?"

"Not like He did."

"No tests?"

"No. But people call their own hardships tests," Sarai explains. "They say that if they make it through, they do so with God's grace."

"What are other things that are God's?"

"God's glory. There is a song even! I heard a mother sing it to her children when she was waking them: 'Rise and shine and give God your glory, glory. Rise and shine and give God your glory, glory. Rise and shine and give God your glory, glory, children of the Lord.'"

Naamah laughs.

"Though I guess there it is the children's glory."

"It doesn't matter—it was worth it to hear you sing that." Naamah laughs again, and it's not quite that Naamah's being rude. Sarai can feel that she is not teasing her. It is that Naamah creates moments of wonder somehow.

In this moment, Sarai hears the song lingering in her ears, and she marvels at it, so different from how she'd felt, when she'd thought of it as almost cruel, to sing to children. She can't bring herself to tell Naamah that the song, as it continues, is about the ark.

SUDDENLY A CHILD runs into the room. "Mom!" he yells when he sees Naamah.

"Shem! Sweetheart!" she says, bringing him into her arms, hugging him close.

"Mom, can I have a plum?"

Naamah stares at his face. It is definitely her son, and yet here, in the future with Sarai, she had somehow forgotten she was a mother.

"Plum, plum, plum, plum, plum," says Shem.

He is so beautiful, and he is smiling at her. She says, "Of course you can," and in her hand is a plum. She gives it to him and he dances off with it. She wants to follow him. She turns to ask Sarai, but she's gone.

Without Sarai there with her, Naamah loses her image of the future. She's spun back to the desert, the cactus in bloom before her again. She can tell there are women nearby because there are always women nearby. They will care for her if she asks. But she can't make it to them. She's still thinking of Shem's small face. She feels a profound guilt that she could forget him for even a minute of her life—the largeness she feels as a mother, the impossible being that a mother is—and so she also grieves her malleable self, how easily she slipped into the role of voyeur, outside of time, outside of her life.

Then the cactus's blossom grows large. It swallows Naamah

whole, pushes her through the fisted hand of the prickling green, and then she's falling through the cactus.

Inside is not the yellow flesh she has eaten, but rather the maze from the underwater cave. Behind her is the large fingertip of a man, tracing her path as it comes to him. She closes her eyes, and when she opens them again she is sitting with Sarai in a small, hard-shelled vehicle with a low roof and windows all around. Through the windows, she can see they are moving impossibly fast.

"There you are," Sarai says.

"I thought I lost you," Naamah says.

In front of them is another vehicle, a box on eighteen wheels, and the hard black road before them curves hard, rounding to the left in two sloped lanes. Next to the road is a sign warning that trucks will fall to the right if they don't slow down. Naamah would have sworn they'd fall to the left, toward the center of the circle.

As if she's hearing Naamah's thoughts, Sarai says, "It's not that the truck falls; it's that the truck wants to continue moving forward, so as the head of the truck turns left, the body follows its own momentum, twisting off to the right and falling away."

"Where did you go?" Naamah asks.

"You left, Naamah. After you saw Shem. I thought you had to do something else. Dreams can be like that. I didn't leave you."

They're entering the jughandle themselves now. Naamah feels her body lean to the right as the driver takes the turn quickly. The car disappears and she tumbles out, straight ahead, as if everything else around her weren't going left, left, left. Naamah's body falls onto the road, rolls up the ramp of the shoulder, and flies into the air. Her body seems weightless as she flies, tracing the straightest line she's ever traveled. Then she crashes into a bird, and another bird, and another, and they cling to her as if she's gathering snow. The birds shriek, and Naamah cries out, too—an imperfect projectile, feathered and clambering.

"Naamah!" a voice yells. It's Jael. "Naamah, stand up!"

She hears him and straightens her knees and raises her hands until her body is stretched and the birds fly away from her. When she is free of them, she lowers her arms.

"What were you doing?" Jael asks.

"I don't know."

"Are you okay?"

"I think so." Standing in the sky feels like swimming, upright but off-balance, off-balance but supported on every inch of her body. She didn't know the wind could feel this way. In fact, she knows it can't.

"What are you doing here, Jael?"

"Sarai found me. Brought me to you."

Naamah looks around until she sees Sarai.

"Hello, Naamah," Sarai says, looking at ease even in the sky.

"What's happening?" Naamah asks her.

"Something's wrong. I don't know what yet."

"Maybe this is Jael's dream after all," Naamah says.

"That's what I've been saying!" Jael says.

"I will see you again, Naamah. I promise," Sarai says, and she's gone.

"What do we do?" Naamah asks Jael.

"If it's not time to wake up—"

"Yes, if it's not time—"

The surface of the world rushes to Naamah's feet. They are back in the desert. Jael, beside her, changes proportions, his rib cage expanding, his legs lengthening and turning knobby, his head becoming almost grotesque, until he is human-shaped.

"Wow," Naamah says.

"I kind of like it," Jael says, the bottom of his giant beak moving into his giant neck as he speaks. He lifts his feet, holds up his wings, fans out the feathers around his head.

"That's nice," she says, grateful for his shade, not realizing how hot she'd been.

He tilts his head, sees the sun return to her face, and straightens it again to shade her. He whistles, his cheeks filling with air, his stiff, narrow tongue moving up and down. "Naamah, do you think I am a woman-shaped cockatoo or a man-shaped cockatoo?"

She looks him up and down. "Neither."

"But I am human-shaped."

"You are more human-shaped than you were."

"My eye is nearly the size of yours."

"Yes."

"My body is immense."

"I know."

"But I am not shaped like a woman, or like a man?"

"You are amazing to look at," she says.

"Am I?" And he grows bigger.

"Yes."

As he grows bigger, she can't help but be afraid of him. He starts to flap his wings. "Naamah," he yells down to her.

"Yes, Jael."

"I can't seem to fly with these proportions," he says. He flaps harder, kicking up dust, creating a wind strong enough that Naamah closes her eyes and mouth. The wind lifts her off the earth again, and her body seems to find the path it traveled before.

"Naamah!" Jael cries after her. "I can't reach you!"

She closes her eyes and tumbles for a long time, until finally she is stopped by the talons of the Egyptian vulture.

"Hello, Naamah." He perches on her arm.

"Hello," she says, opening her eyes.

"Do you remember me?"

She nods. "You're the Metatron." There's blood on her arm from his talons.

"Apologies. I can't help that," he says.

"It's okay. It doesn't hurt."

He moves his foot, smearing the blood.

"Sarai said there was something wrong with my dream," Naamah says. "Is that because of you? You've been trying to get me alone?"

"You know, when I look at your head, I'm reminded of an egg, and I want to drop a rock onto it over and over until it cracks."

"It is you, isn't it?"

"I have opened eggs this way hundreds of times. I wedge the top of my beak into the crack and hold the egg steady with my foot and snap off more of its shell."

"You don't scare me," she says.

"I've lost a good bit of the liquid inside with this method, watched it spill into the hot sand. But I get most of what I want."

"Are you listening to me?"

"Sometimes," the Metatron says, "it takes me quite a long time to find the right rock for the job."

## SEVENTEEN

Noah and Naamah wake up early and take a raven to the deck. Noah hesitates. "What if it comes back with a hunk of flesh in its beak?"

"It won't. I've been swimming all over and seen nothing, come across nothing."

"Okay," he says, and he lets the raven go.

It flies out and lands on one of the mountaintops near the boat.

"It's already stopped," he says.

Naamah laughs. "A little less eventful than we thought, huh?"

But then: "Look! Look!" Noah says, as the raven takes off and flies into the distance. And Noah's excitement is so great that Naamah follows his direction. She looks out across the water for a bird she cannot see.

SADIE COMES UP TO THE DECK. "What are you two doing up here?"

"We sent out the raven," Naamah says.

Sadie looks around, checking each horizon.

"We haven't been able to see him for a while," Noah says.

"When do you think he will come back?"

"Not sure," Naamah says.

Sadie keeps gazing out, in one direction and then another.


LATE THAT NIGHT, Naamah wraps herself in a blanket and takes a small bowl of nuts to the deck. She lies down next to it and falls asleep.

She wakes up to the sound of the raven's beak knocking around in the bowl.

"Weren't you gone a long time," she says, sitting up.

As she listens to the raven work on a pistachio, she takes out her sharp bone and scrapes a patch of hard, thin skin off a doum nut. She sticks the point of the bone into the flesh and traces it down, twice. She drags the flat of the blade down between the lines and takes out the slim rectangle of the spongy fruit.

She tears a bit off, places it in her palm, and extends her hand toward the raven's tapping. She feels his beak take it. With her other hand she puts the rest of the fruit in her mouth. Sweet and sour. Bitter and spicy. She likes how much work and time it takes to have such a small bite.


THE RAVEN FLIES back and forth for days, until Naamah no longer follows his comings and goings. One night, Noah stays on the deck.

He says that when the raven comes back that night, he will return him to his room.

Knowing she'll be alone for a while, Naamah takes out a long stone, polished smooth and slightly curved. She places it between her thighs to warm it, and until it's warm, she thinks of it only as a rock.

WHEN NAAMAH WAS A CHILD, her mother would peel half a doum nut and give it to Naamah to gnaw on, to keep her busy. Naamah remembers the feeling of her teeth scraping on the pit. It distracted her longer than most things could.

When she was becoming a woman, her mother didn't have to tell her about sex. Naamah had seen her parents together one afternoon when she was supposed to be out, and another couple under a juniper tree she passed going to the river early one morning, and two men once in a tent near the market.

But her mother did tell her about the desire she would feel. When she should let another person fill that desire and when she should fill it herself. And her mother gave her the long stone that day.

WHEN THE STONE IS WARM and ready, Naamah thinks of Bethel. In the desert, Naamah's neck was so warm that it matched the warmth of Bethel's mouth. Bethel understood this. She would take Naamah's neck in her mouth. Then she'd blow on the wet skin until it rose in bumps. Then she would lick it again, and that time Naamah would feel it.

Naamah reaches down and moves her fingers inside her vagina until they're slick. She rubs them over the stone and then she puts the stone in. She lets it fill her. She takes her other hand and rests the tip of her middle finger on her clitoris. She wants her body to tell her what it wants next.

She goes back to the memory of Bethel and her finger moves—first down the inside of her labia on the left, then down the right. She starts to move the stone and she moves the other hand around to the bottom of her ass, the top of her thigh, and she grabs it hard like Adata had. She imagines both women with her now, and the angel, too.

She doesn't need to move fast. She just needs to get the placement right. When her body rises to bursting, she stops the stone, raises it toward her stomach, the whole length of it, until she gasps, and then she pulls it out and her body is lost to her orgasm.

She rolls to her side and pulls in her legs as if she could trap her orgasm, observe it in the folds her body can make, thighs against stomach, arms over shins. She imagines it as a glowing thing, like a small globe of honey.

Adata and the angel drop away, but she can nearly feel where Bethel would be, lying in the bed.

ONE NIGHT, while walking in the halls, Naamah hears Neela laughing. Naamah tries to open the door quietly, but Neela notices her right away.

"Naamah, Naamah, close the door," Neela says, waving her into the room.

Naamah closes it. "What are you doing?"

"I took out a jerboa, and boy, he can jump."

Naamah laughs and sits next to her along the wall. "Have you done this before?"

Neela nods. "When it's hard to sleep, I walk, and one night I found this room. It gets so noisy at night with the nocturnal animals. I came in and saw the jerboas and their burrows in the sand, and at first I wanted to feel the sand. Just feel sand again. But then one came over to my hand, and it let me pick it up. I took it out and it raised its whole body off the floor, balancing on its tail, and I clapped for it. It jumped to almost the ceiling, and I clapped again, and laughed and cheered for it. It doesn't give me any trouble about putting it back. I think it likes me."

Naamah listens, watching the baby moving under the curve of Neela's belly.

"I don't think the baby is ever still for even a second anymore," Neela says.

"I didn't mean to stare."

"It's okay. It's amazing."

Naamah smiles.

"It's been hurting," Neela says.

"Are you worried?"

"No. No, it's been hurting the way women say it hurts, low across my belly. But in waves. It doesn't arrive and leave, like I've seen in women who are going to give birth."

"Your body is practicing."

"My mother took me to births so I would know what it's like."

"It's normal," Naamah says.

"And soon I will have them like the other women did?"

"Yes, and then it will really be time. Then the baby will come."

"I'm so excited, Naamah."

"Me too."

"You're not mad? That I'm having a baby on the ark?"

"No. We will make it work. We're all so excited, I think."

Then Naamah feels something land on her head.

Neela starts laughing. The jerboa moves this way and that on Naamah's head of black hair. Neela laughs harder and harder. "Oh," she says, "I'm going to pee myself." She laughs harder and places her hand low on the side of her enormous belly.

"Well, just go over to that bucket and pee if you need to."

"Right in front of you?"

"Oh, I don't care," Naamah says, trying to figure out how to get the jerboa off her head. She leans forward, hoping the jerboa will just jump off, but it doesn't.

Neela pees, and she keeps laughing, watching Naamah's efforts, so her pee stops and starts until she's finally finished. She goes over to Naamah and lifts the jerboa off her head, and then, slowly, untangles the hair that's gotten caught in the jerboa's toes.

"Thank you," Naamah says, wondering what the jerboa looks like in Neela's hand.

"Thank *you*," Neela says, still smiling, still amused.


NOAH THINKS it's time to send out the dove. Naamah has wanted every day to send out the dove but has held her tongue, wary of her own eagerness.

"If it doesn't return, it has found a place to build a nest," Noah says.

"I know."

"I know you know," Noah says, smiling at her. "I'm nervous."

"What's there to be nervous about? If it comes back, we wait a week, we send it out again. The water has to go away at some point."

"You would think," he says.

He looks most attractive to her when he's making small, sly jokes like these. And when they're having sex.

THIS TIME they all go out on the deck together. They release the dove and celebrate. They cheer and dance and drink.

Noah and Naamah leave the children to continue. They go below deck, and it's warm enough that they undress before they get into bed. Naamah curves her back into his chest, and at first it seems like they will go to sleep. But then Noah begins to move his hand up and down her side.

Naamah takes a sharp breath in and arches her neck to signal to him that she's ready. He kisses her neck. She can hardly feel the kiss until it's over and the air touches her skin. She arches her back next, to raise her ass to his groin, where she feels his soft hair and his erect penis. He slides his hand down below her legs and touches her everywhere he can before he lifts her leg and slides in. Noah takes his time, gaining speed.

When Naamah's close to orgasm she says, "Get on top."

He comes out and they change positions and she guides him in again and grabs him with her legs, her knees high on his sides. She watches his body move into hers. She doesn't know why that action turns her on—it's not much to see—but it does. As he gets faster, she stops watching, brings him closer and bites his shoulder. She slaps the flat of her hand on the back of his ribs at the same speed as he moves into her, then twice the speed. She feels like she's going to pee, but she knows she won't. And he's about to orgasm. And then he does. And then she does.

Even as he softens, her orgasm continues around him.

"Should I come out?"

She nods.

When he does, her orgasm comes on more strongly, but only for a moment, and then it subsides.

"I'll pee first," he says.

She laughs at the waves of her orgasm as they continue to come, if infrequently. Then she gets up. She kisses him on his back as he pees into a bucket. After he finishes, she pees in the bucket.

"I'll take it out," he says, and picks up the handle.

"Thank you," she says, and she crawls into bed, the warmth of sex already starting to leave her.

## EIGHTEEN

In the morning, Neela comes to Naamah and Noah's room. She looks concerned.

"What is it, Neela?" Naamah asks.

"The mucus came out, this morning. And I haven't been to bed. The pain comes on and ends with—as if it has edges."

"Then it's soon now."

"What should I do?"

"Walk if you can."

"That's it?"

Naamah nods and smiles at her.

"Should I wake Ham?"

"If you want to."

"Maybe not yet."

"Okay," Naamah says. "After breakfast, we'll prepare everything."

"It will be that long?"

"Yes, I think so."

But Neela doesn't leave.

"Do I look worried, Neela?"

Neela looks at her and shakes her head.

"Then okay then. Everything is okay."

Neela nods. "Okay. See you at breakfast."

"See you then," Naamah says.


AT BREAKFAST, everyone is excited except Neela. Neela looks like she's going to be sick. But she keeps smiling at people and telling them she's all right. Sadie offers her food, but Neela refuses.

Adata and Naamah start to collect water. They stretch a thin cloth over the biggest basin they have, then pull up bucket after bucket of water and pour it over the cloth. The water is the cleanest they can get it. They peel off the cloth, and Naamah takes it down the ladder to the floodwater, rinses it and wrings it out. Adata fills the basin of clean water with smaller cloths.

Japheth and Shem drag clean hay up to the deck to make a soft place for Neela. Naamah never kept birth from any of her boys, so they know Neela will wreck the hay with blood and fluid. They know they'll need to drag up fresh hay again and again. They are happy to do it.

Noah grabs the little wood stool they leave with the cows and the one they leave with the milking goats. He brings them up to the deck near the hay.

Ham and Sadie stay with Neela as the pains come more quickly. Ham has fallen silent and looks ashen, but he holds Neela's hand firmly. Sadie encourages Neela to bounce, or to put her knees in the hay and push into one of the stools with her hands. But Neela doesn't want to move anymore, doesn't want to move at all.

THERE WAS A TIME when Naamah had a cough that made her feel like her only job in the world was to avoid moving, in case it made her cough again. If she hadn't coughed for a minute, she'd freeze in place. Her breath would grow shallow. And she'd know she needed next to nothing to continue in this world, alive.

But she also knew that taking shallow breaths let the depths of her lungs grow wet. So then she'd try to breathe in, in the same way as her shallow breath, but for longer, until her chest filled up, like a rabbit that had eaten the wrong thing and was swelling with gas. It would work for a few breaths, but then one would catch and she would cough again.

She would feel the cough all around her ribs as if it could change her shape. It made her sweat, and the sweat stank. She didn't normally smell much when she ran or worked, but this was a sick sweat—like an animal's, but with the sharpness of an herb.

"DO YOU WANT TO LIE DOWN?" Naamah asks.

Neela looks like Naamah has granted her a wish. Ham helps her roll onto her back.

"You still have a ways to go," Naamah says.

"Do I have to get up again?"

"No, of course not," Naamah says.

Another contraction comes on, and Neela makes one quick sound before she's silent with it, clenching everything in her body. Ham runs his hand up her clenched forearm to her fist. She doesn't look at him. And then it passes and she relaxes. She takes his hand.

"I don't want to get up," Neela says.

"You don't have to," Ham says. He kisses her.

"Look," she says, looking over his shoulder. Everyone turns to look.

The dove is perched on the railing.

"That's got to be a good sign," she says. "Like a blessing."

Ham kisses her again, smiles at her.

*Maybe*, Naamah thinks. But even if it's a good sign for the baby, it's not a good sign for the world the baby's about to be born into.


IN THE EARLY DAYS ON THE BOAT, Naamah spent a lot of time with the dogs. They liked to play fetch and other games Naamah would make up. One day, after they tired themselves out, Naamah lay down in the mess of dogs. They all panted, and as she rubbed the belly of the one near her hand, she felt a lump in the fur of its belly.

At first she thought little of it, but the next day she went back and checked the dog's stomach again. And there the lump was. Naamah worried over it for a short time, and then she decided to trim the fur, to have a better look. As she dragged her sharp bone over the fur, the lump became more pronounced. Without hesitating, she sliced right down the middle of it. She pushed on each side of it and nothing happened. But she noticed then that the lump moved. She could have sworn it moved.

She couldn't think what else to do but put her mouth to it. As soon as the vacuum was made, the larva came into her mouth and she spit it into her hand. She hated the feeling of its squirming in her hand so much that she grabbed the larva with the cloth of her dress instead. She had to run out of the room, telling herself she couldn't feel it through the cloth, telling herself she'd done the right thing.

NEELA'S WATER BREAKS and it runs down, toward and over her anus. The contractions get worse. "I thought I wanted the baby to come out," Neela says, "but now I don't know. Maybe the baby shouldn't come out."

"What do you mean, Neela? It has to come out," says Ham.

"I don't think it does. No. Does it, Naamah?"

"I think you'll be happier once it's out," Naamah tells her, trying not to laugh.

The next contraction comes, and by the face Neela makes during it, Naamah can tell: "You're close now."

"I'm ready," Neela pants. "I'm ready to try another position."

Ham helps her get up on her knees. She rests her bent arms on the stool and hangs her head over it until her forehead touches it.

"Does that feel better?" Naamah asks.

"It does. The pressure is down more. Off my back."

"That's good."

"I think I should push now. It feels like I should push."

"Okay, Neela." Naamah looks up to Noah. "You'll have to lift her and help her lie back once that baby starts to come out." He nods.

Neela looks up at Noah. "Will that be okay?" She looks back at Naamah. "Will that hurt?"

Noah leans down. "Not at all, Neela."

Another contraction comes. "Push," Naamah says, holding her hand against the base of Neela's vulva.

Neela makes a low, steady sound as she pushes. "Did I do it right? What should it feel like?"

"That was a good first push. Really good."

"I don't know how it should feel."

"It feels like shitting," Naamah says.

Another one comes and Neela pushes again.

"Try to relax, Neela. It's just that one place you have to push."

Neela's embarrassed. "I think I might have diarrhea."

"That's okay. That's normal."

And on the next push, Neela craps into the hay beneath her. Adata quickly moves it away, pushes it off the side of the boat. Japheth puts fresh hay in its place. Sadie hands Naamah a clean, wet cloth, and Naamah wipes Neela, front to back.

"That feels good," Neela says. "Can someone put one on my head?"

Ham rushes to grab another cloth from the water. He folds it and drags it carefully over Neela's forehead and face.

"Just put it on my head. The whole thing," she says.

So he unfolds it and puts it over her head. He tries not to cover her face.

"It's fine," she says. "It feels good." She closes her eyes beneath it.

Another contraction comes. Neela doesn't need direction now. She pushes as hard as she can.

"Hold back, now," Naamah says. "That's good." She covers her hand in oil and holds it to Neela's vulva again. She wants to make sure everything is soft and pliable. She holds firm against the skin that will tear if given the chance.

As THE WEEKS passed on the boat, Naamah returned to the dogs less and less. The dogs grew more sluggish, happy only when they were leashed and led around the deck, and who could blame them. One day she noticed another lump on one of them, and this time she would not risk having to put her mouth against it.

She fed the dog valerian root. She shaved the hair down until the skin was bare. She sliced along each side of the lump and peeled an almond-shaped piece of skin off. But underneath was not a worm. It was clear and springy, and as she pulled it out and sliced it off, she found more, and she pulled and sliced that part away, too. And as soon as it was gone, she noticed the dog had other lumps, the same type, harmless, all over its body.

She sewed up the wound with needle and thread, cleaned up the fur and blood as well as she could, and hoped no one would discover what she'd done. She felt ashamed because she knew her anxiety was already getting the better of her.

WHEN NEELA PUSHES AGAIN, the head begins to show, bowing out Neela's vulva, a shape gained only by birth.

"I can see the head," Naamah says. "Covered in hair already."

"Go look, go look," Neela says, knocking Ham on the arm.

He goes around to look. "I see it, Neela."

Another contraction comes. "Big push now," Naamah says.

With it, the head is out. Noah takes Neela from under her shoulders and lifts her and pulls her back in one smooth motion until she's lying back in the hay. Naamah keeps her hand under the baby's head, and it's so steady, as if Neela's body were orbiting a tiny red sun.

"Again," Naamah says, "hard as you can."

The shoulders come out and the rest of the body falls out fast, like it's made of liquid. Naamah puts her mouth over the child's nose and sucks out the fluid and turns her head to spit it out. She wipes the baby's face until it's clear, lays the chest of the baby on her leg, and hits the baby's back twice. The chest fills with air, and when it empties again, the baby screams out.

Naamah cuts the cord with her bone.

"Is it a boy or a girl?" Neela asks.

"It's a girl," Ham says.

"I want to hold her."

"Not yet, honey," Naamah says, handing the baby off to Sadie. "Lift her up, Noah."

"Oh no, Naamah, I can't stand," Neela says as Noah gets her to her feet.

"He'll hold you the whole time."

"I will," he says.

"You have to push out the placenta now, okay?" Naamah says.

"Okay," she says, but she's looking at Sadie, who's wrapping the baby in a dry cloth. The baby has already stopped crying.

"Look at me," Naamah says. "This is important."

Neela looks back at Naamah with some anger in her eyes, knees weak beneath her.

"Then you'll get to hold her," Naamah says.

Neela nods.

"I'm going to pull a little on the cord as you push, but you tell me if it hurts."

"It all hurts, Naamah."

"If it hurts differently."

Neela nods again, and when the contraction comes she pushes it out. Noah lets her fall back toward him and gets her settled in the hay. Ham moves to sit behind her so she can rest against him. Sadie hands the baby to her and stays seated next to them. Naamah investigates the placenta and makes sure it's whole. Then she lays it down on the deck. It falls flat, almost like a mushroom cap, but wet and heavy and loose.

"All there?" Adata asks.

"Yes."

"Then it's done."

Naamah looks at her, but she's still thinking fast, still feeling like she might have to jump to action, save someone, sacrifice something.

"You got her through it, and it's done now," Adata says.

Naamah relaxes. "Yes," she says, and she looks over at the child's face. Her skin is as brown as a star anise. "What will you name her?" Naamah asks.

"Danit," says Neela.

"Beautiful," Naamah says, and she nods at Ham.

He smiles back but finds it hard to look away from his baby girl. "Can I hold her, Neela?"

Neela lets him take her into his arms.

"Hello, Danit. Hello, little one."

"Can we all hold her?" asks Sadie.

"I want her back with me," says Neela.

"If she only gets used to your smell, Neela, she'll never let you put her down," Naamah says.

"Then I want to hold her again between each of you holding her."

"We can do that," Sadie says.

Ham kisses Danit on her forehead. The child receives hundreds of kisses before the day is through.

LATE THAT NIGHT, Naamah takes the placenta down to the tigers' rooms. She takes a chicken with her, too, holds it by its feet.

The tiger that Naamah fed the lamb to never settled. Noah and Naamah have both heard the sounds of claws and snarling. They stopped allowing anyone else down near those rooms. They would rather do the extra work of cleaning and feeding themselves, rather than worry.

Now Naamah hopes that this meal settles the tiger once and for all.

As she approaches the row of tiger rooms, the tigers begin their chorus of rumbling. She opens the empty room, which gets covered and cleaned of blood over and over. She dumps the placenta in the room, releases the chicken, and then leaves again.

When she pulls on the rope that raises the small, square, heavy door between the rooms, she can hear the tiger's body move from one room to the next. She lowers the door slowly so it doesn't spook the tiger. Then she enters the other door to clean the tiger's shit and replace the hay, so that the room might still smell of grasslands.

The chicken lets out a peal of clucking, and for a second Naamah mistakes it for a woman's voice, laughing outrageously, as if at someone's expense. The sound scares Naamah more than the tiger's sudden silence.

When she's finished cleaning the room, Naamah settles by the square door between the rooms and listens through it. The tiger extends a paw and then puts it back. Her shoulders are the highest point of her body, her head and haunches held low. Naamah can't hear anything at all when the tiger stalks like this, but she can hear the chicken peck at the placenta.

And then the tiger pounces, ends up clear on the other side of the room, allows her back to bang into the wall, and Naamah lets out a tiny cry. She can't help herself. If Naamah had been able to see the tiger, and had blinked right then, she would have thought the chicken disappeared.

## NINETEEN

The whole family spends a week taking shifts, bringing the hungry child to Neela wherever she is on the boat, waiting for the child to finish nursing, then taking the child, burping her, holding her over a bucket to shit, rocking her back to sleep. Sometimes not in that order. Sometimes one of them ends up with the runny, yellow shit on their arms, spit-up on their shoulders. Sometimes one of them cycles the baby's legs until a tiny burst of gas escapes her anus and she settles again.

After a week, Noah wants to send the dove out again. They gather on the deck. Neela lays the baby on the raised beds of grass Naamah has grown. Neela strokes Danit's cheek and tells her how beautiful she is. Danit's head turns toward her mother's hand, her mouth rooting for it. She makes a face as the blades of grass poke her cheek.

"What is that?" Neela says, smiling. "Is that grass?" Then she hears Noah talking to the dove.

"Bring us something back this time," he whispers.

Neela sits up straight and almost yells, "Bring us something back, dove!"

Naamah laughs, and they all start cheering on the dove. Noah releases it, and Danit cries at their loud voices; they've been so quiet around her for every day of her life before this. Now they quiet themselves again.

"Go on," Neela says, scooping her up. "Don't stop on our account. I want her to know what excitement sounds like. Don't I, little girl?"

But no one knows what to say. They can all tell the water is significantly lower now, but they still haven't seen one tree. They have only their hope to send with the dove. And their desire to get off the boat.

NAAMAH WONDERS how Danit would turn out if they were never able to leave the boat. Before long they would have to let out all the dangerous animals, all the animals whose hungers they couldn't satisfy, all the birds it seemed cruel to keep. Many would drown. Or some would kill each other and others would drown. Or some would kill each other and some would drown and then maybe one or two would starve on the bloody patch of ground beside the boat. And then Naamah would clean that up, too.

Danit would be like any other child. Naamah admits that to herself. She sees her running up and down the halls of the boat. She sees her hiding in the small rooms and pretending she is somewhere else that she cannot name or describe. She sees her in the connected rooms, playing with the square door, pretending to escape something else she cannot quite picture.

Naamah wonders what they would teach her about the world outside the boat. Together, would they think to spare her from what she would never know? Or would they work to build up the world as it was and as it could be? Maybe they would remake every empty room into a place she might have had on land. One a temple. One a market. One meant for an empress. She can see Noah constructing a bed with ornate posts that reach the ceiling.

It soothes Naamah to imagine the ways they might redirect their energies if they had no animals to care for. But would God be rid of them, too, if they let the animals die? She thinks eleven months has been a long time to tend to the animals, enough to earn their reward, especially if the reward is only to be left alone. But to Him, what is eleven months?

"How LITTLE SHE DOES, Naamah," Neela says, looking at Danit.

Naamah laughs.

"When will she do more?"

"Not for a while."

"She is darling, though."

"She is," Naamah says.

"I thought I'd be so excited to show her everything. Teach her words. Let her touch fur and wool. But none of those things would mean anything to her right now."

"They will."

"I have met babies before," Neela says. "How did I not remember?"

"You said it yourself. What's to remember? Except maybe exhaustion. And you were so much younger then."

Neela asks, "What was Ham like, as a baby?"

"He was warm. Always. The other babies needed to be bundled, but not him. He slept easily, with his limbs sprawled, as if he were comfortable in the world from the moment it embraced him."

"Danit's not like that."

"No. Most children need to be wrapped, to mimic where they have been, to transition. To give them time for their backs to grow large and flat, to support the whole of them."

"But not Ham."

Naamah laughs. "I guess not. But it didn't feel strange because he seemed happy. And that seemed lucky to me."

"I think he will be a wonderful father."

"I'm sure of it," Naamah says, though she knew saying otherwise would be admitting a failure on her part.


NAAMAH AND JAPHETH are looking out over the water. Everyone else is asleep. Everyone's been so tired with the baby on top of their regular chores.

"Adata wants to start trying," Japheth says.

"Does she?"

"She thinks we'll be off the boat by then. That the timing will work out well."

"And you?"

"I'm nervous," he says. "And not about the boat."

"What, then?"

He gives her a look. "About repopulating the earth."

"It's a lot of responsibility if you think of it that way," she says.

"How do you think about it any other way?"

"Should I not have had you, knowing I'd be making you the patriarch of a nation?"

"But you didn't know." He looks upset.

"I know. You're right." She puts her arm around his waist and lays her head against his shoulder. "If there's anything I wish for you, it's that you have your family and all the joy you can possibly have in life. To not overthink it. Because no matter what our lives could have been, every version would have been filled with shit we'd have to deal with."

And then the dove comes back. It flies right to Naamah, landing in front of her on the railing. And she sees only a leaf, floating in the air as if from God Himself.

"What is it?" Japheth asks.

"An olive leaf, I think." She takes it from the dove.

"Do you grow those on the boat?"

She shakes her head.

"Mom," he says, "what do we do?"

"Let's wait for morning. I'll wake your father when I go down, and if he thinks otherwise, I'll come get you."

"It still looks covered in water."

"I know, but don't—don't be that way."

"What way?"

"I don't know. You're forgetting how surprising the world can be."

"This coming from the person who goes around for days as if you've given up."

Naamah doesn't respond at first.

"I'm sorry," Japheth says.

"No. You didn't hurt me. I know what I've been like. But you misunderstand. If you look at all this water and distrust the olive leaf, you're forgetting how little you know. You're thinking yourself more than you are, and yet using that to belittle yourself and your life and the world. When I can't stand the boat anymore, it's because of how little I know; it's because of the smallness of my life against the size of the world."

"You're contradicting yourself."

"I'm not trying to," she sighs. "I use my understanding of the un-knowable world to call myself to be unique and wondrous *among* its wonders. I don't become arrogant about what my eyes can see and what I can understand. I don't dismiss myself or my life either. I don't know, Japheth. I don't know. Look and see: you're right—there's no land to live upon. But also, look at the olive leaf."

Japheth takes the leaf from her. "The thought of a tree—"

"A tree," she says.

NAAMAH SHOWS NOAH THE LEAF. He says it's good news, but as he's falling back to sleep he also says it means there isn't a place to stay. "There's not a better home than the ark. Not yet."

Naamah falls asleep holding the leaf.

AT BREAKFAST, everyone is buzzing. People start narrating life on land to the baby for the first time. "Stiff shrubs that one day burst into bloom. . . . Stalks of plants with tops like shredded fabrics, except lighter than air, as if they'd fly off if it weren't for their green stalks. . . . Mud that comes up between your toes, and a river that washes them clean again." Danit takes it all in, everything and nothing. Her breath is noisy. She snorts and gurgles and wheezes and holds her breath and starts again. She is conspicuous with living.

## TWENTY

Deep below them, on the lowest deck, the tiger still has not settled, and Naamah is at a loss. Food has always worked. The animals were nothing if not predictable. Or they had been. She doesn't know if she should tell anyone, not when they are all so happy and excited. But maybe that's what has unsettled the tiger. Maybe the tiger can tell the promise of land is close.

NAAMAH GOES TO THE ROOM of paintings and searches for one of a landscape of the tiger's own habitat, where her stripes would hide her well. Naamah finds one that's good enough and takes it down through the boat. She's already let another chicken into the room for feeding. She's let the tiger listen to it and wait. When she comes back, she opens the square door and hears the tiger pad through. Naamah can tell how silent she would be if she weren't on planks of wood.

While the tiger eats, Naamah sets the painting up in the room of hay, directly across from the square door. Then she nails a board across the square opening so that the tiger will be able to see the landscape, but not pass through. She leaves and waits for the tiger to finish eating.

She sits against the wall and cleans her nails, dragging her left thumb under each finger on the right, her right thumb under each finger on the left, and then her middle fingers under each thumb, until the movement looks almost like she is making something, like she can spin a thread from her skin. She is so lost in the repetitive action that it takes her a moment to realize that the tiger is panting by her ear, on the other side of the wood, pressing up against the wall so she might be heard.

It could be to intimidate Naamah, and she does feel intimidated, but it could just be so that Naamah opens the door back to her other room. It could be that the tiger is trained, as much as a predator like her can be trained—a reluctant acceptance of a learned situation.

Naamah wonders, *If she understands so much, does she understand the flood? Does she know she is being saved? Does she remember the other tigers and know they must have drowned? Does she know drowning? Does she know God?*

Naamah stands and opens the square door. As soon as she does, the tiger goes to it. She fusses with the plank before she spots the painting. Naamah can almost feel the tiger seeing the painting, as everything goes quiet.

Suddenly the tiger runs across the floor and pounces at where Naamah is standing. Naamah hears her raised paws hit the wall near her head, and she is so startled she drops the door. It slams and the tiger roars. Not one of the low rumbles, but a terrible roar that shakes every animal on the boat into response. Naamah runs to the deck, leaving the painting and the tiger where it's eaten, surrounded by the smell and stains of her kill.

"WHAT'S HAPPENED?" Noah catches her in his arms as she runs up the last set of steps.

"I upset the tiger."

"How?"

"I showed it a painting and then it scared me, so I dropped the door and I scared her and she roared and she scared everything else."

"What do you mean you showed it a painting?"

"I . . . I'll have to show you."

"Okay."

"Right now?" Naamah asks, still shaking.

"No. We can wait until they all settle back down."

"Thank you," she says. And they sit down and wait.

NOAH AND NAAMAH REMOVE the nails and take down the plank of wood together. They take the painting out and then let the tiger back into her room. They leave the painting in the hall while they clean the eating room as best they can, of blood and feathers and chicken shit, anything that might make the tiger think some new prey is nearby. Then Naamah takes Noah to the room of paintings.

"Who brought these?"

"Neela."

"Neela?"

"Yes. She painted some of them herself."

Noah pulls a stretched canvas toward him, and then another, and another, looking at portraits and landscapes and scenes from the market and of people bathing—a record of the old world.

"What is it?" Naamah asks.

"Will He punish us for these?"

"Why would He?"

"People will know of things they might not have known, of a world that no longer is. That was not supposed to be."

"He didn't tell us we couldn't speak of our past."

"But paintings last longer than any story we might tell." He runs his fingers over a naked figure. "They are nostalgic in a way that cannot be helped."

"It's better to have them." Naamah tries to catch his eye, but he won't look at her. "If He doesn't like them, He can burn them once we're off the boat. But He won't burn us. We're all He's got left."

THE WEEK CRAWLS ON AS they wait for the day they'll release the dove again. The tiger is still a mess. Naamah wonders if she should let another tiger in with her. While pacing the narrow halls, she hears Sadie crying in her room. Naamah opens the door without knocking and rushes over to her.

Sadie grabs onto Naamah and pushes her head into Naamah's stomach.

"It's okay," Naamah says.

"I don't want to die."

"You're not dying."

"I don't want to die ever."

"Okay, Sadie. It's all right."

"I don't want to! I don't want to!" Sadie yells.

"It's not bad, Sadie."

Sadie won't stop repeating, still mumbling, "I don't want to! I don't want—"

"You keep going, Sadie. Even afterward."

Sadie stops at that. "Do I?"

"Yes. Of course you do."

"But without my body?"

"In a way."

Sadie is panting. "I like my body."

"Let's go up in the sun."

"No!" Sadie finally looks at her. "I don't want anyone to see me like this." She lies back on the bed, not touching Naamah, curling away from her.

"Has this happened before?" Naamah asks.

Sadie nods.

"Does Shem know?"

She nods again.

"What helps?"

She shakes her head and hard sobs come for her again.

"Should I stay?"

Sadie doesn't answer, so Naamah lies down next to her and holds her until she stops heaving.

"Can I do anything?"

"It just passes," Sadie says.

"Okay. I'll stay with you."

———

SADIE TRIES TO TAKE a deep breath that doesn't break on its way out. On the fourth breath, she does it. "Talk about something we'll do later. Something tangible."

"Tonight we'll have dinner together. You'll hold the baby. I can make you something hot to drink. You can help peel a carrot. You could swim."

Sadie's calming down.

"You know, there's a tiger who's feeling a lot like you right now."

"Really?"

"I've been trying to figure out how to help her, but maybe I should have been asking you all along." Naamah laughs how she always does. "I'm thinking she might need company. Do you think I should let in another tiger to see her?"

"Maybe."

"Should I let in a male or a female tiger with her?"

Sadie can't speak again.

"I was thinking a male could be nice. They might have sex, and maybe that feels good for tigers, right?"

Sadie laughs.

"But a female—maybe they would comfort each other."

"She could hurt her, if she really feels like I do."

"Do you think so?"

Sadie nods. "Him too."

"You're right." Naamah sits up. "Any ideas?"

Sadie sits up, too. "Valerian root?"

"I could try that." She smiles at her. "Are you feeling better?"

"Yes. It's over."

"What's it feel like?"

"Terrible," Sadie says, "like all of my skin is being pricked. And my vulva feels like it's on fire."

"What?"

"I know. And it's not burning or anything. It's just like the pin-pricks are more concentrated there, so concentrated, like it can tell where it's flesh instead of skin, and if I had time to think any other thought, I would think, *What is happening to me?* But I don't have time."

"I'm so sorry it happens."

"Has it never happened to you?"

Naamah shakes her head.

"It doesn't usually get that bad. I can usually think of something good, something to look forward to, and it will stop. But today it didn't work."

"It's hard to know what we're looking forward to right now."

Sadie doesn't say anything.

"Not that I'm not looking forward to getting off the boat. I am. But I couldn't describe what it's going to be like."

"I know," Sadie says. "We shouldn't talk about it."

# TWENTY-ONE

After dinner, Naamah makes a tea for Sadie with valerian root. She pours it into a cup, and Sadie thanks her and takes it off to bed. Naamah knows that's not strong enough for the tiger. She decides to try to make something with poppy seeds. She gets them from the cold, quiet room at the bottom of the ship. It's less cold now that the water has receded.

She brings out two stones, one large and flat and another in the shape of a smooth cylinder. She places the seeds on the flat stone, adds a little water, and starts to work the cylinder over the seeds. As they turn to paste she adds more water, little by little, as it holds together. But she's worried the tiger won't eat it.

She puts the paste in a bucket and adds water to the paste until it breaks. She swirls her fingers through it, checking for clumps in the dark, and then she takes the bucket to the deck to leave it overnight.

In the morning, the water has begun to evaporate. She tells everyone not to touch the bucket, that she's making something for one of the bigger animals. She goes below deck and she removes the tiger's water from her room—that way she might want it more when Naamah returns it to her later. And while it makes the moaning of the tiger worse that day, echoing through the boat, Naamah thinks it's worth it.

After all day in the sun, the water in the bucket is gone. The residue is thin along the wood, and Naamah scrapes it off with a spoon, not with her bone, so that none of the bucket comes with it. She hopes the tiger won't notice the flakes in her water. Why would she?

NAAMAH DOESN'T WANT TO give the tiger too much, but too little would be a wasted effort. She can't stand the thought of trying yet another thing and still being left with a tiger clawing and dissatisfied. And haven't they been accommodating? Couldn't they have made the animals' rooms smaller, more cagelike? Made them live on grates so their shit fell through and they'd never have to be moved at all? Let all their muscles atrophy? She thinks, *Haven't we been the miraculous people we were chosen to be?*

So maybe Naamah overdoes it with the flakes in the tiger's water. Maybe she does. And maybe it's only that it's been another long day after so many long days in Naamah's life. But next she hears the tiger's body fall down with a soft thud, as if from buckled knees, and soon Naamah can't hear her breathing.

She rushes back to the seeds. This time she grabs the ephedra seeds and gets to work on a paste. When she's finished, she takes the paste and a bowl of water, goes to the tiger's room, and opens the door. It's the first time she has opened a door with such a large predator behind it, and she is scared.

As Naamah moves into the room, shuffling her feet, it crosses her mind that perhaps she should let the tiger die. Enough of the other animals have died for one reason or another. And the other tigers are doing well. In fact, she decides, she should leave. Of course she should leave. That's when she feels her toes in the tiger's fur.

She places the bowls on the floor and finds the tiger's head with her hands. Then she moves the bowls closer. She opens the tiger's mouth and puts the paste down her throat. Then she pulls the tiger's head onto her lap and pours water into her mouth. And then, blind to everything that matters in the room, with the tiger's head heavy on her bent legs, she thinks she's killed the tiger. She strokes her under her chin.

"I'm sorry," she says.

But the tiger snaps awake, curls its body, and springs to its feet, clattering the bowls and splashing water. Naamah jumps up, acting on instinct, and runs for the door. She tries to slam the door behind her, but it doesn't slam. It hits the tiger's body. Usually Naamah would take pleasure in that kind of sound, new, singular to a door hitting a tiger, this tiger. But she is focused only on running away, on making it to a door she can barricade.

The tiger reaches her first, tackles her to the ground. Naamah is thrown face-first onto the floor, the tiger's breath on the back of her head. She uses all the courage left in her to roll over. She wants, at least, to face the tiger when she dies.

The tiger's head flashes into her vision and out again. In and out. Never staying. It looks the way the angel looked during sex that day. And then Naamah realizes it: that was a warning, a premonition; the angel is only the angel. Naamah begins to cry. Why did she cling to one reading of the vision? How arrogant she is. And now the angel scorned, and herself brokenhearted. She thinks, *How absurd I am to exist at all.*

The tiger places a paw on her head, turns it until Naamah's cheek is on the wood. Naamah feels the animal's claws dig into her skin, one behind her ear where there's no hair, two in her hair above her ear, and one in her cheek, which cuts deepest, with no bone below to stop it. Then the tiger roars so loudly that, even though Naamah's ears are covered, she feels the sound through her head, feels it shake the roof of her mouth. Other tigers start to paw at their doors and walls.

"I'm sorry," Naamah yells.

At this, the tiger seems to stop.

"Look around! You're out now. There's nowhere to go. When there's somewhere to go, I will let you go. I'm trying to get you there." Naamah stops yelling. "That's what I'm trying to do."

The tiger makes her long, low sound, as if she's trying to throw her voice across a desert. She takes her paw off Naamah's head, and Naamah turns to face her again, even if she can't see her. The blood from the cut on Naamah's cheek runs down to her ear. She hears the tiger's body shifting above her, shifting her weight so she might raise a paw and strike Naamah.

Right then the tiger comes into perfect focus, as if Naamah has been able to see her all along.

The sight of the tiger makes Naamah so happy that she wants to grab her, pull on her fur, scream. The tiger hisses, and Naamah sees the wrinkling above her nose to the inner corners of her eyes, her whiskered face rising over teeth until her cheeks are as perfectly round as a child's. Naamah likes infantilizing her this way, to make her less terrifying.

Naamah covers her neck with her arms, knowing the tiger will go for that first, and she hisses back at the tiger. But it doesn't make her feel powerful. If anything, the sound, sparked from the back of her throat, emphasizes her hopeless body.

But then, in an instant, the tiger flies into the ceiling above her, whimpering as her back hits the beams. Then the tiger flies backward, toward its door. Then she's dropped. As if she gets the message, she goes back into her room.

Naamah sits up, and the little blood that made it to her ear runs to the bottom of it, the thinnest red coating, like a glaze on a cake.

When she looks up, she sees the angel coming through the wall, rushing toward her. Out of the water, she emits that exceptional light again.

"Are you all right?" the angel asks.

Naamah nods.

The angel looks only into her eyes, as if she might see, through them, any other injury.

"Thank you," Naamah says. The angel kisses her, but Naamah doesn't kiss back—her fear of the tiger hasn't left her completely. She says, "We should close the door."

"The tiger won't be a problem again."

Naamah keeps her eyes on the doorway.

The angel says, "I promise."

"What was wrong with her?"

"She hates the boat."

"She doesn't care that I hate the boat, too?"

"No."

"Would she have killed me?"

"Yes."

"Eaten me?"

"Probably not. I think she was planning to make an example of you—tear off all your limbs and leave your headless torso at the bottom of the stairs."

"Okay, okay, that's enough detail." Naamah laughs and takes her eyes off the doorway, finally looks at the angel. "Wait, what was she going to do with my head?"

"I'm not sure."

"And God would not have stopped her?"

"No."

"Did He think about stopping her?"

"No."

"If He had thought about it, do you think He would have stopped her?"

"I did."

"No, I know that."

"I didn't mean it that way. I don't need recognition. I mean, when I thought about it, I thought to stop her."

"How did you know it was happening?"

"I could feel you both."

"What have you done to her?" Naamah asks.

"I'm distracting her."

"What do you mean?"

"It's like I'm giving her a dream."

"What's the dream?"

"That she's in the jungle. That she's crossing streams. That she is happy."

Naamah shakes her head. "She won't be happy to come back here, after a dream like that."

"In the dream, she'll be called by God to the ark, and she'll come. She won't remember the months she's already been here. And she'll be thick with His message for long enough."

"You're sure?"

"She really scared you, didn't she?"

"My heart is still racing."

The angel reaches out her hand. "Do you want me to slow it down?"

"No. It's all right," Naamah says. "Is the water shallow?"

"Much more shallow. Not where we are, but on my way to you."

"You are all okay?"

"We are."

"And you will stay there?"

"I think I will," the angel says. "And I want you to come back with me."

"When?" Naamah asks.

"Now."

"I can't come now. Maybe in a few years. Could I come then?"

"You could still come," the angel says. "But I can't know what will change between now and then. Neither can you."

"Would you still love me?"

"I don't know."

"Don't you experience time differently? Wouldn't it all pass more quickly for you?"

"Yes, but I experience your rejection again and again, don't I?"

"And you are so sensitive?"

"I am. If that is the word you choose."

"But can't you understand my commitment to this? My children and grandchildren?"

"I understand it. I have turned my back on commitments myself."

"If I come with you now, I will not be able to love you. I will worry over what I have left. I will hold it against you."

The angel is quiet, but Naamah is getting worked up, taking quick breaths and lurching forward as if she could convince the angel, with only the slant and forcefulness of her body, that the angel wants something different from what she's already made clear.

The angel says, "I could give you anything you want. I could take anything you want away from you."

"I can't. I don't want you to do that, like you did to the dam."

"I won't ask you again. I won't save you again. I can't keep seeing you."

"I understand."

"You are okay with this being the last time we see each other?"

Naamah shakes her head. "There's nothing I can say. Or if there is, I don't know it. I'm not the woman you think I am. I mean something only here."

"You think that—do you hear yourself?"

"If you made me feel otherwise, I wouldn't trust it."

"You ruin yourself, Naamah."

———

NAAMAH TAKES THE ANGEL'S HAND. "Won't I be happy here?"

"You will be. I can't deny it. You will have so many grandchildren, and you will create nations. You will feel such purpose and you will find a happiness in that purpose because you always do. You will be happy."

"Will you be happy?"

"My life is not so easily seen."

Naamah kisses her hand.

The angel climbs on top of her and kisses her. She kisses her over and over again. She takes Naamah's lips between her teeth. She lets Naamah suck on her tongue. Every kiss is some new ratio of their lips, tongues, and teeth, given and received, removed so they might be given again.

Naamah can't believe the weight of the angel's body. And yet she feels no pain from it. She feels for the first time how the angel, de-spite taking on this female form, is far larger than she appears—massive, in some form of matter Naamah cannot see. She knows she can love the angel, but she's surprised she's allowed to kiss her. She moves her hands over the angel's dry arms. She moves her hands to feel more of her body, to slide her hand down the center of her stom-ach. But as soon as she does, as soon as she reaches her stomach, the angel is gone. As if Naamah touched a button that released a trap-door and the angel fell through it, straight down, maybe straight through Naamah. And Naamah is alone. And the animals are silent. As if each and every one of them is dead.

## TWENTY-TWO

The day arrives when they want to send out the dove again. The water seems low, and new parts of the mountains have been revealed, with green grass and knotted plants that will surely flower soon into great sweeps of purple and yellow.

They don't cheer this time. They don't chant their wishes at the bird. The bird flies off and they all watch until it's out of sight, even Naamah, who can see every animal again. She wonders if it remembers the way to the olive tree, if it will be happy there.

This time, if all goes well, the bird will not return. And while its disappearance could mean a great many things—that the bird has died, for instance—they will have to take the absence as a good sign.

Naamah can't think of many times in her life when she has greeted an absence with faith. Perhaps the absence of blood when she and Noah were first trying to get pregnant, when she couldn't say, before then, if she were a fertile woman.

———

Naamah expects Adata to start their preparations with purpose, but she keeps to her room.

"What's wrong?" Naamah asks.

"I made promises to you, Naamah. Promises that were easy to make on the ark and with life on land in the future, some future no one could make out. And I'm worried I can't keep them. Now that it's here—all here, all of a sudden."

"You mean, your life with Japheth?"

Adata nods.

"Have you been happy here with him?"

"I have."

"Why would being on land change that?"

"I don't know. On land I could run away."

Naamah laughs. "Just go one day to the next."

"There is a safety to the ark."

"Is there?" Naamah asks. "Listen, Adata, if months from now you are not happy with Japheth, then he will not be happy with you, and the two of you will be unhappy and you will have to find some resolve to that, and it will not be your fault; you will not have betrayed me or this family or God. That is life."

"That is life."

"Yes. Now help me figure out what we should eat before we leave and what is worth carrying with us."

Adata follows her down to the lowest floor of the boat, which still holds a chill. "The tiger is not growling," Adata says.

"No."

"Is she dead?"

"No—no, of course not."

"We have all spoken of the marks on your face, Naamah. But we were afraid to ask. I didn't think of what could have made them until now. Did you meet the tiger?"

Naamah touches the scab on her cheek with the tip of her middle finger. "Yes."

"How are you alive, Naamah?"

"I don't know," Naamah says.

At the storage room, they lift boxes to see which are the heaviest. They consolidate vegetables that had been stored separately, when there were more of them. They move boxes to the hall, for what they'll want to eat soon. They don't remark upon how strange every action feels, in what might be their last days on the boat.

AFTER A WEEK, Noah agrees that it's safe to say the dove will not return. Noah was the last holdout. And while they all knew he would come to think this, their newfound agreement invites a certainty that surprises everyone.

That night Naamah can't sleep, but to her surprise, neither can Noah.

"We have so much to do," he says.

"I know."

"Should we make a list? Should we assign tasks?"

"We can if you want to," Naamah says.

"Would you do it?"

"Have Adata do it. She needs something to be in charge of right now."

"Why? Why do you say it like that?"

"Nothing. She's just anxious, like you are, wide awake when you should be asleep."

"I guess we're all on edge," Noah says.

"Except Neela. She's too tired to be on edge."

"Are we not helping enough?" Noah asks.

"I don't think it matters what we do. She has to eat and her body has to draw on itself to make milk. Even if she were sleeping perfectly, she'd be exhausted."

"I remember when you were like that."

"You do?"

"Yes. You could fall asleep anywhere. We would be down by the river washing clothes, and you'd say, 'I have to lie down for a second,' and then you'd be asleep in a patch of grass, a baby next to you on his back, looking at the undersides of leaves and swatting at his own legs."

Naamah laughs.

Noah kicks off the blanket the way a baby would.

"Noah!" Naamah gasps.

He laughs and grabs the blanket and pulls it up over both of their heads and kisses her on the nose. "Remember the tents we would build with the boys, with ropes and blankets in the branches of tamarisk trees?"

"Yes," Naamah says. "Now let me out of this thing." And she pushes the top of the blanket down and tucks it under her arm. "I'm going to sleep," she says, closing her eyes, but still smiling.

"I'm going to do that with our grandchildren," he whispers.

She puts her hand on his arm and they both go to sleep.

LATE IN THE NIGHT, Naamah wakes and lies in bed and wonders whether the boat offers safety, as Adata suggested. A sameness. A containedness. Yes. A vessel that demands a certain repetitiveness of the body. When was the last time Naamah jumped to reach something? Or crawled under something? She cannot remember—everything here is so perfectly made for humans, for herself and these seven other humans specifically. They made so many decisions so quickly as they built, or as they were surprised by something they'd forgotten. So many adaptations.

Then Naamah hears a note of some kind, almost giggling, as if something delightful might be expected. Yet as she follows the sound, she cannot guess what the delight might be.

She climbs down the ladder to the patch of land, which has grown in size, big enough to hold an entire market. She walks out to the edge of it, to the water, closer to the sound, and spots a glimmer farther out. Thinking it might be the angel, Naamah rushes toward it, still in her clothes. When the water reaches her waist and her clothes begin to float up around her, as if she's begun to blossom, she realizes it is not the angel but the children who have come to see her.

"Hello, children. What are you doing here?"

But she can't hear them. All she can hear is the same sound she heard from her bed.

She crouches down under the water, feels the film cover her

mouth. She knows the angel will be able to tell she's entered the water again.

"Naamah! Naamah!" the children clamor. "We heard about the tiger."

"I see the mark on her face."

"I see a cut behind her ear."

One child begins to comb through her hair.

She says, "That's enough, children," but she still lets the girl comb through her hair for her scabs. "Please tell me how you've all been."

"We've been well."

She turns to one of the boys. "And you, how is your mother?"

He looks down at his feet. "She is fine."

"Have you all been to the cave? To see the art she has made?"

"No, we haven't."

"Well, you must. Don't you care for the adults down there at all?"

"We care for you, Naamah."

"I know."

The children tell her stories of how they've explored the world the angel has made. One has brought a crystal with him and shows how he has learned to change its shape himself. He is so proud, as if he might grow up and be an angel one day, if only he learns how.

"Tell me why you have come," Naamah says. "The angel must not approve."

"We didn't tell her," one shouts.

"We heard about the baby," says another.

"The baby?"

"Oh yes! And we wanted to know when we would see a baby, and the angel said we might never see one! So we had to come!"

"I see."

"So can we see the baby, Naamah? Please."

"I don't see why not. If you are quiet and unseen."

The children nod.

"Come with me, then."

"No," the children say, stepping back, deeper into the water. "We can't leave."

"You'd have me go get the baby and bring her to you?"

The children nod and move closer again.

"Wait here for me," she says.

Naamah stands again and feels the air rush over her skin, sees the moonlight. She could simply forget the children were there. That's how discrete their worlds are from one another.

STOPPING IN NEELA and Ham's doorway, Naamah spots the baby asleep between them, wrapped tightly in a blanket. She goes to the side of the bed where Ham is sleeping, knowing he is less likely to wake, and she lifts Danit from the bed. No one stirs.

On the deck, she wraps Danit to her chest with a swath of cloth, and in this new position the baby snores.

Naamah climbs down the ladder, walks across the new land, and wades into the water. As the water creeps up toward the baby, Naamah unwraps her and tucks the end of the long cloth into her waist belt. It unfurls from her hip. She holds Danit in her arms.

The children motion for Naamah to come closer. She holds the child high and lays her own ear to the water.

"She's beautiful!" one says.

Another yells out, "Can we touch her?"

All the children pause at that, and then they all repeat it, louder and louder.

Naamah stands up abruptly. She stares down at Danit, still asleep, still swaddled. She doesn't think the children can hurt her, but she doesn't know. She doesn't know if, on her own visits, the angel protects her from the touch of the children. She doesn't know much about the dead at all.

The night is quiet, the air cold, the children merely a shifting light on the water, as if they reflect the moon more than the surface of the water does. Naamah undoes one corner of the blanket and Danit's arm falls out. Naamah feels the skin of her arm, softer than any animal on the boat. Danit squirms and her hand reaches out. Naamah thinks just to touch a finger to the water.

As Naamah leans toward the water, the baby's hand hanging from her body, the undone wrap pouring off her like a song would, if a song were a fabric—it is at this moment that Naamah hears a wild scream, and she stops.

Neela is wailing on the deck, leaning over the railing.

Naamah stands up and walks back toward her. "Neela?" Naamah climbs to her, holding Danit to her chest, letting the wet cloth trail behind them.

When she reaches the deck, Neela bursts into tears and grabs Danit from her.

"Are you okay?" Naamah asks.

"I'm not hurt, Naamah. I'm furious."

"With me?"

"What were you doing with her?"

"I just—" Naamah tries for an explanation that doesn't involve dead children. "I was showing her the water before it's receded."

"She's *asleep*, Naamah. We were all asleep."

"The water is so different at night."

Neela shakes her head. "And me waking and not finding her, how did you think I would react?"

"I didn't think you would wake."

"Have you taken her like this before?"

"No! No."

"How can I trust you?"

"Of course you can trust—"

But Neela cuts her off. "There are only so many of us, Naamah!" And she cries harder and shoulders past Naamah, going back below deck.

Naamah goes to the railing and looks to see if there are still shining spots in the water, each the head of a dead child, waiting for her.

# TWENTY-THREE

In this dream, Naamah is charged with the care of a baby much like Danit. The infant keeps escaping her somehow—Naamah's left her in the sun, she's abandoned her by a ledge. Naamah runs to her, saves her, holds her tight, kisses her on the forehead, promises not to leave her, and then the child disappears again. It would be torturous if not for the nature of dreams.

This time, they are both on the side of a volcano that has erupted, the ash cloud above them, not yet settling, so everything is dark but clear. And while they are both in danger, the baby is closer to the lava, which moves slowly enough that it seems like they have a chance. Naamah lifts her up and runs away, down the slope. Her breath is ragged and her legs tire. She wants to look behind her to see if she can rest, but her head won't turn.

Her feet kick little rocks, and they bounce out in front of her, hitting other rocks, making sharp sounds for the last time before the lava takes them. Her feet land on rocks in ways that make her wince, that make her muscles spasm. Her feet keep moving despite herself, until she wonders if she is not a machine made only to *think* that she requires food, water, breath.

Behind her, the lava pushes forward in its red lush. A gray peel creeps up its edge, a reaction from touching the ground below, a brief cooling, and then the gray splits into a dozen thin crescents, one after another, as the red pushes through, as if globular in its essence, or in the essence of its motion.

And then the Egyptian vulture is there. Naamah stops.

He asks, "Do you know why my head is bare?"

"No," Naamah says, catching her breath.

"It shows how deep I might insert my head into the dead." He turns to allow her to admire his head in profile.

"Not as deep as other vultures, then?"

He huffs.

As much as Naamah enjoys that she's bothered him, she wants him to leave, she wants this thing with him over. "Did you want to tell me something?"

"No. God wants to speak with you."

Naamah notices that the child is gone from her arms. The baby is at the Metatron's feet. He lifts a foot and puts it on the blanket wrapped around her.

"Don't hurt her!"

"I would not." The Metatron looks straight at Naamah. "Now, if she were dead . . . "

"She's *not dead*."

"She's not alive," he says.

"Yes, she—"

"You are dreaming, Naamah."

Naamah looks left and right as if that might confirm something. "So what? So what if I am? Is that what God wants to tell me?"

"No."

"Then tell me already. Tell me!" she shouts.

But before he can begin, everything disappears around her.


NAAMAH LANDS in the desert again, and Sarai is there, holding the baby.

"Do you want her back?" she asks.

Naamah nods and takes the baby. "Thank you." She checks the blanket for signs of the vulture's talons. "Where did he go?"

"I took you. He is still there."

"He had something to tell me. Something God wanted to tell me."

"And you want to hear it?"

"Yes. Of course. Shouldn't I?"

Sarai doesn't answer.

"The angel said God didn't care about me. Was not watching," Naamah says.

"The angel has been away."

"So He does want to talk to me?"

"He does."

"Do you know what He wants to tell me?"

"No, but I think I would want to spare you from anything He might say."

"I think I need to hear it."

"It will change you, Naamah. Remember how Noah was changed?"

Yes, she remembers the first day Noah talked to God. He came home and it was like the wind had been knocked out of him. He told her that His voice seemed at home in the expanse of the world, but thinking back on that voice, once he was in *their* home, near her, close to what he'd considered the heart of his life, the voice seemed overpowering, dwarfing everything he held dear. He dropped down to the floor and muttered, *What is my life?* The feeling left him the next morning, but Naamah remembers it still. She couldn't understand how their love could be made small. And yet Noah had made a point of it—that she should know that his love for her would never devastate him again, that he would never again look at her across the desert, thunderstruck.

"I remember," she says, "but we made it past that. I like where we are now."

"That was because of your work, don't you think? Would Noah know how to do the same for you?"

"I wouldn't go through those feelings. I already know my place. And I know how contemptuous He is."

"You shouldn't expect to be able to tell Him anything, Naamah, or to ask a question."

"Okay, Sarai, but I still want to hear it."

"I don't care," she says. "I won't let it happen here. And if He can't do it here, He'll have to do it when you are awake. And then you won't be left wondering if it was real. I won't let you have those questions on top of the questions you will already have."

"Fine. When I'm awake, then."

"But Naamah," Sarai adds, "you have to remember the dream."

"What dream?"

"This dream, Naamah. Me. Jael. The Metatron."

"Jael," Naamah says, alarmed. "Where is Jael?"

"Find Jael. He will help you. He is on the boat. You know this. You have found him there before."

"I don't remember."

"I know. You must bring the worlds closer. You must know one from the other, but bring them much, much closer."

"What about the baby?"

"The baby is not real. You feel guilty that you almost let the dead children touch Danit."

"I remember that. Would that have harmed her?"

"Yes."

"Then I'm right to feel this way." The baby in her arms doubles in size.

"It didn't happen. That's what matters. Besides, the children have a greater pull than you might think. They have their own power. Forgive yourself quickly, as there's much to be done. The worlds are closer already."

"Okay," Naamah says.

But Sarai persists. "Forgive yourself now!"

So Naamah thinks, *No harm came to her. You know better now. You did it, but you will not do it again.* And the baby vanishes. Naamah's left with a blanket draped over her arms.

"Find Jael," Sarai says. Then she's gone.

Naamah imagines the dreamscape as a world that can spin as fast as a child's toy. She takes a step and crosses mountains. Three steps across the ocean and her feet splash all over the world. If she must find Jael, surely she will reach him this way.

AFTER HALF THE WORLD has passed, Naamah decides to change direction, walking straight through the North Pole. The water on her feet freezes into thin ice, cracking off again with her next step. As she approaches the equator, the sun catches her on the bridge of her nose—and there is Jael.

"Naamah!" he yells. He flies into her chest, and she wraps her arm around him, bending it up over his body. He bites at her fingertips.

"I saw you on the boat," he says. "You didn't recognize me."

"I'm so sorry, Jael. Sarai says I have to remember you."

"I will try to help," he says.

They walk across the world together now, not saying a word, until the sound of her own footsteps becomes unbearable.

"I've been thinking," she says, "about what makes a woman."

"You have?"

"I don't want it to depend on being a mother, even if it has for me. I don't want it to depend on genitals. I think very little of a man's genitals. But with my uterus comes my period. It's not just how my life is marked, how I experience this monthly reminder that I am this body and not another—and monthly is *so often*. But there are choices I make, and others make, because of it. How one woman sometimes turns away from another. How we deal with how much it hurts, if we decide to speak it. How we deal with the blood.

"But I think we all know we could be women without these choices. The only reason I've ever wanted to be a woman is to have children. The only reason I did not feel constant anger at my body's insistence on itself was that I knew I'd have my children one day.

"I have no interest in womanhood. In any particular dress. In any particular tasks. In any particular voice. I don't want to be a man either. I want a new form."

"You could be a bird with me."

Naamah laughs. "Would I be happy, do you think?"

"I do. I do."

Naamah runs her fingers over his head.

"Naamah, when a cockatoo is pregnant, she must lay her egg. But I've heard that humans can stop their pregnancies."

"Yes."

"Have you ever done that?"

"I have. I took herbs that a woman gave me."

"Did it work?"

"Yes. But it hurt. For days."

"Why did you do it?"

"I didn't want the child. That's all that matters. When I had my boys, everything was right then. That's how I know I made the right choice."

"Naamah—"

"No more questions, Jael."


THE WORLD STAYS SMALL, Naamah's steps colossal. She realizes she's spent this whole dream cradling one body and then another. She lets Jael go, and he flies around her as she ties her hair up above her head. He perches there, talons clutching her hair instead of her skin. She looks like a queen with Jael as her crown, and he spreads the feathers around his head as if he understands this.

Clomp, clomp, clomp, the queen spins the world.

NAAMAH STOPS IN THE DESERT. This is how the world looks when it's not flooded, she remembers. And quick as that, the flood returns, up to her ankles. The trees are gone, the mountains, the canyons, everything. When Naamah's still, the waters are still. She leans forward to see her reflection. Jael does the same.

"Impressive," he says.

"I'll say."

A voice comes from overhead. "You look like a woman with a bird on her head," says the Metatron, circling above.

Naamah whispers to Jael, "We cannot let him speak."

"All he does is speak."

"Well, then, we can't listen to what he has to say."

"You don't need to whisper," the Metatron says.

"Do you enjoy a little rotten fruit sometimes, vulture?" Jael asks. And as soon as he says it, and she thinks it, rotten fruit rises to the surface of the water.

"I have already eaten and will not be distracted this time."

The smell of the rotten fruit begins to reach their noses.

"I don't know how to escape him," Naamah says.

Jael yells, "Why is your head yellow?"

"I don't know," the vulture answers. "I never have reason to look at my own face."

"Look in the water now," Jael says.

"No, you listen to me," the Metatron says, but just the same, he flies low to see his yellow head in the reflection of the water.

"Jump," Jael says to Naamah.

She jumps, and the water splashes up into the air, casting waves high as her knees, and the Metatron is caught by them. He flails his wet, feathered wings.

"Will he drown?" Naamah asks.

"It's only my dream," Jael says. "Or yours."

But she can't stand the sight of him like that, the black tips of his wings like fingers. She reaches down and saves him, blows a gust of wind toward him that's so warm and dry it takes every lick of moisture from him, and from most of the earth. Naamah is standing in the desert again, towering above the sand.

The vulture flies up to her face. "That was very untoward of you both."

"You deserve worse," Jael says.

"You could not mean less to me if you tried, cockatoo. I don't know how else to make this clear."

Naamah laughs. She sits down in the desert and lets one leg dip into a sea, lifts the other leg so that her heel rests on the canopies of a rain forest. She runs a fingernail through the soft sand of a beach. "Maybe we can ignore him," she says.

But the birds are focused on each other.

"I don't do this for your attention," Jael says to the Metatron.

"I think you do. What if I offered you a place with God? I can give that to you."

"What do you mean?"

"I mean you don't need to return to the ark. You could enter the house of God and be one with Him."

Naamah looks at Jael.

"I am not even considering it," he says to her.

"Do you believe him, Naamah? Or did he take too long to answer? Have you lost all your trust in him?"

"Is that what you've come to tell me, too?" Naamah asks. "Are you here to offer me something?"

"No—"

"No!" Jael says. "Don't let him say it, Naamah." Jael flies up to the vulture and attacks him in the air.

They both throw their wings back and lift their feet to tear at each other.

Naamah moves her leg in the sea and sends a tsunami over the land. She moves her other leg and the trees of the rain forest fall beneath it. She lies back, feels the world's soft slope under her, and watches the birds fight. *It's a dream*, she tells herself, her love for Jael aching inside her as she watches. But the Metatron is right. She will never feel quite the same about Jael again—all the loved ones God could take from her, in more ways than death.

Jael has scraped the vulture under his eye, and the Metatron bleeds.

Tense, Naamah presses her fingers into the earth, carving new canyons. When she lifts her fingers again, her nails are dark red at their tips. She brings them to her mouth, scraping the clay out with a front tooth that runs crooked to the others.

The vulture tears himself free from the fight, blood staining his white ruff. Seeing Naamah lying there, he flies inside her, up through her vagina.

She sits up and then bends over her stomach.

"Naamah!" Jael yells. "Are you okay?"

She brings herself to her feet and vomits.

"Naamah!"

She lifts her head as her chest swells with air. When she opens her mouth, it's the Metatron speaking.

*"You must hear me, Naamah! You must listen!"*

Naamah spits the last of the vomit from her mouth. She digs her toes in beneath her, and the earth allows it.

Jael flies around her furiously. When she opens her mouth again, he flies into it. It's all he can think to do. He knows he could choke her like this, that his talons might tear into her as he clamors inside, but he hears the voice of the Metatron trying to rise inside of her.

And she will not listen. She doesn't even need to fight the vulture. She knows so simply that she will not listen to him that she wakes from the dream.

## TWENTY-FOUR

The water is all but gone now. But the family doesn't spend time on the land, as if none of them trusts it yet. Instead they start to dismantle the boat. They remove the roof and reassemble the ramp the animals once climbed. With it, they are ready to let even the wildest animals find their way back off the boat. But that's not how they begin.

First they let off the smallest animals. The ones who take a single slice of fig and make it last forever, as if time has stopped moving, as if their mouth could not possibly be capable of feeding a body; those animals whose survival suggests that life itself is meaningless, if one animal can be so brazenly ineffective at living. Or at least this is how Naamah has grown to feel about them. If they choked on their food, it would be a miracle of their tiny throats.

But honestly no animal has choked in more than a year on the boat, and Naamah wonders if choking is mostly a human thing, an aggressive impulse to eat and speak at once. Naamah recalls times she's choked on her own spit.

As they release the animals, some head back toward the boat, some even start walking up the ramp, but Shem chases them back down. Naamah understands the appeal of the familiar. She understands, as she looks out across the land and its little growth, the appeal of the shadow.

The family waits a week before releasing any other animals, before the birds, the snakes, the cats. Soon they will no longer worry about these prey animals—they will hardly even think of them—but for now, they are giving them a chance.

THEY BUILD WAGONS from the rest of the roof, the railing, and parts of rooms they've emptied. They will need to carry food, animals that tire along the way, animals they'll need for eggs, milk, and wool. More than anything they'll need wagons to carry wood, to give them all they need before the trees start flourishing again. Naamah hopes they can tear the boat down to the ground, taking apart every piece of it, as if it never existed.

WHEN THEY CHOOSE A new place to settle, Naamah knows, they will choose it based largely on its proximity to water. Part of her wants to stay on a mountaintop and melt snow when she needs it. Part of her would be happy to go the rest of her life without seeing another body of water on the earth.

But that would only solve things for her, alone, if everyone else should die again. A prospect that never feels beyond what He might do. She tucks away the idea of her mountain home, in case she is spurned, and spared, again.

She turns her mind to planning the ecosystem of their new home, just as she planned their lives on the boat. Which animals, which plants, where to put the tents, where the water, what paths they might make from one thing to another. For a woman sentenced by God, Naamah is surprised by how often He allows her to take a god-like role.

THE PREDATORS ARE MORE CONFUSING. The snakes have to be let out before the birds because the snakes are prey to the birds. And the smaller birds are prey to the bigger birds. Timing it all is so overwhelming that Naamah wonders if it will ever be done.

On the day they release the cockatoos, one stays behind, perching on Naamah's shoulder. When she brushes him away, he flutters nearby, then returns.

She pushes him off her shoulder. "Go on," she says.

But he will not. "Jael," he says.

"Jael," she repeats.

She holds out her hand and he perches there, clinging precariously to her fingers because it's clear that's what she wants. They look at each other for a long time.

"Well, if you must stay, do your best not to bother anyone," she says. "And that includes me." She laughs.

Jael can tell she doesn't remember, but he's determined to be nearby when He reveals Himself to her outside the dream.

# Naamah

---

EVERYONE GROWS FOND OF JAEL. Naamah keeps nuts in her pockets for him, which is not surprising, but so does Noah, who sometimes gives Jael a perch as well. Being around them all the time, Jael learns new things to say: *Hello* and *Dear one.*

Soon it is time to release the larger animals. They kill a horse and cut it into as many pieces as they can, so they don't have to kill more. They hide most of it in a room filled with hay and Naamah's most fragrant plants. They lay a small trail of meat from the bottom rooms to the ramp, leaving blood between the pieces. And then they hide themselves in the fragrant room, Japheth and Noah holding makeshift weapons, Adata and Ham barricading the door once everyone is inside.

They do this for the bears, the panthers, the tigers, one enormous animal after another, quiet on their padded feet. They keep resetting the trail with fresh meat. They think it will take two days, but they keep having to stop for Danit's crying, and it helps all of them to take breaks, to spend time in the air.

Naamah is shocked at how the world, large as it ever was, seems more tenable now, seeing the land, dipped and heaped, ever-varying, instead of looking over the endlessly flat water. The world seems smaller simply by how her eyes take it in.

ON THE THIRD DAY, A brown bear strays from the path and finds their room.

Naamah peeks at it through a crack. She had been frustrated for so long by her inability to see the animals that she's able to accept the bear, in all its glory, without a flinch. She takes in every hair, and if she thinks of God anymore, she thinks of Him as the infinite number of hairs over the bear's body. Some have caught dust, some are shorter than others, some are not hairs at all but whiskers.

But that's not quite right. Does she think of Him rarely, or is it always?

The bear wanders away.

EVENTUALLY THE BOAT IS CLEAR. They are left with wagons, boards, plants, seeds, dried fruits, and vegetables still in sand. Neela must tend to Danit, so only seven of them can drive the wagons and the carts they will pull behind them.

Naamah works among the half-destroyed rooms of the boat—a piecework village of her own, fittingly mislaid compared to that of the angel's making.

She goes through each piece to make sure they've missed nothing, but even in pieces the boat still smells of animals and their piss and shit. As she steps through it, she says to herself, *This is the last time I will see these rooms. This is the last time I will smell this smell.*

When she stumbles across one of the overhead door pulleys from the rooms of a dangerous animal, she twists her head around, as if one might still be beside her, and she dislodges Jael from his perch.

"Dear one," he says.

She laughs. "I'm all right. Just spooked myself."

"Hello," he says.

"Don't worry," she adds. "We are quite alone, aren't we?"

And it's true, the rest of the family is elsewhere, tending to other things, to the docile animals. The carnivorous animals are gone. She wonders where they have all disappeared to, what new homes they have found.

ONE NIGHT, she wakes from a dream and she can't help herself. With Jael on her shoulder, she walks out to where the angel lives. It takes a long time to find it—well into the next afternoon—everything made unfamiliar by the air. It's a lake now, and her first thought is to dive in. But she knows that if she sets even a toe in the lake, the angel might kill her. Such is the anguish of a woman who has made herself clear. Even this close, the angel might feel her. And the children she cannot trust anymore.

She turns back.

AS SHE RETURNS, Noah sees her first and runs to her across the land. She watches his steps, the placing of his feet through patches of new growth.

"You've been gone for nearly two days." He's trying not to raise his voice at her, even though no one is near enough to hear. This is a habit from the boat that they no longer need. Soon they will reacquaint themselves with yelling, with moaning during sex, with the sounds they'd taught themselves to contain. Naamah feels more free just thinking about the sounds she might make. She likes thinking about the word *alone*.

"I'm sorry," she says.

"Where were you?"

"I was scouting out a place we might settle."

Noah wasn't expecting such a practical answer. She had practiced it on the long walk back. He shakes his head as he thinks. "And was it a good fit? Could we go there?"

"No!" And though she had practiced this, too, the *no* still rushes out of her as if she might eat Noah, pluck him right off the earth.

He notices, but says calmly, "That's too bad. Should I scout in another direction?"

"I will do it," she says. She tries to smile at him, but when it comes out forced, she nods her head to hide it. And the action of nodding, some small motion forward, feels like permission to walk past him.

He follows a few steps behind as she walks back to the remains of the boat. She imagines him watching her, wondering what kind of woman she will be on land. And he is watching her, her steps, the same way she watched his. He notices the movement of her hips as her foot lands on a raised rock, like climbing a stair, but with an ease to it, her body moving only forward.

At first he thinks it's new, a whole new curve of her body, but then he remembers. It is not new, but a thing that's returning to her.

So Naamah makes a habit out of scouting, hiking for days, away from the boat and back. She comes to anticipate the day she will travel far from the boat and not look back, a day she sees so vividly now, in such specific detail: how the wagons look, what animals remain, the new baby, Sadie's humming. Even the exactness of the sight of the land feels as if it is about to fall into place.

First, she decides to head away from the angel, toward the rising sun. But at the end of the day, she has passed no water and has instead stumbled upon more mountains. She returns home to eat, refill her water, and tell of the quiet land.

The next trip is similar. More bare land. No water. Mountains ahead.

Soon it frustrates her, how often her path leads to land that cannot take them. How can the earth be free of all that water and not be ready for them, in any direction? And then she feels ashamed at how quickly her human arrogance pulses in her again.

Soon there are trips that do not end in mountains. On one trip, she thinks she sees a lake, very far ahead, but it would take too long to walk there. Noah would be upset at her absence. And he's grown to trust her more with each trip, grown less worried. When she tells him about the lake, he suggests they keep looking, instead of allowing her a longer trip. "Better to find a river," he says. And he's right.

So many of her next trips end in desert that she wants to return on horseback to where she thought the lake might be. But Noah encourages her to continue. She wonders if he wants only to tire her, which isn't the worst idea. She wants to tire, too. Maybe she would wake to some ambition besides survival.

Eventually a walk takes her to the largest lake she's ever seen. When she stands at its edge, it reminds her of the flood, and she panics. She falls to her knees, into the lake. The water hits her face and she grabs at her clothes in the water. She sees a fish dart around her legs. She breathes in and out, focusing on the feeling of the mud until her heart stops racing.

She returns with news of the large lake as if it were a great discovery, but Noah still wants them to continue until they find a river. Again he offers to do a trip himself.

"No," Naamah says, but she's not sure why she insists.

FINALLY NAAMAH FINDS A RIVER. It's not terribly far from where the angel is, but it feels far enough to keep her from wandering there. And the river is extraordinary. Some parts still, some rushing forth, some wide and some narrow, some banks rocky and some so slight she wonders how the water does not overwhelm them.

Then there are the hot springs. They let steam off, curling into the air, reminding her of the roundworms falling out of the horse's intestines, how she'd imagined them. Naamah undresses and steps in. She closes her eyes. She imagines her life becoming a most beautiful thing. But that includes a vision of herself surrounded by people— people who died and people who will never be born. It nearly breaks her.

THE FAMILY CELEBRATES THE NEWS of the river the night Naamah returns. They build a fire bigger than they've built in a year, bigger than they need to, because they can. And they bring out all the wine. It's too heavy to bring with them anyway. Everything has been weighed and judged. Everything is prepared.

As they dance and sing under the stars, Naamah wonders why it feels more appropriate to be raucous at night. The sun is its own glory; they would look stunning beneath it in their joy.

Naamah walks around the fire until she finds a spot where a light wind blows the heat at her constantly. It hurts her skin even though she is at a distance where she can't be hurt.

Jael leaves Naamah's side for longer than he ever has. He flies around each member of the family, his eyes catching the light of the fire.


NAAMAH WANDERS FROM THE GROUP, drunk and happy. *When else will I know all the land around me, in all directions, so well?* she thinks. *Never.*

She doesn't know what to call most of the plants she sees, but she's pleased by their growth. "Well done, you green trouble!" she yells out.

Ahead of her she sees an Egyptian vulture, shining in the night. She stops, wondering whether to change course. She looks at her arms to see if she is shining, too, if it is only the moonlight, but she is as dark as the night.

"Hello, Naamah," the vulture says.

Naamah looks around. "Who are you?"

"I am the voice of the Lord."

"No, you are a vulture."

"That, and the voice of the Lord."

"You," Naamah asks, "are a thing of divinity, vulture?"

"I am. I am the Metatron."

"I've never met, never touched a divine thing. Unless I am one, or the animals—"

"You are not."

"May I touch you?"

The vulture nods.

She runs her fingers over his ruff of feathers. As she touches them, her dreams return to her and she recoils.

"Jael!" she yells. "Jael!"

Her family does not hear her, but Jael does.

"Naamah, calm down," the vulture says.

"You could have come on any hike, all these days, but you wait until now, when I'm drunk and alone, when the light plays tricks on me. Sarai was right."

"I am the voice of the Lord, Naamah. I came to you when I was able."

"Bullshit."

He opens his wings and grows large, closes them and returns to his normal size.

Naamah staggers back from him, and Jael nearly flies into her. She turns and gathers him in her arms. "I'm so sorry I didn't remember," she says.

"Dear one," Jael says.

The vulture says, "Can we begin?"

Jael wants to attack him again, here in the real world, but Naamah holds his wings tight to his sides.

"Go ahead," she says.

The vulture raises his beak in the air and then lowers it. "Hello, Naamah," he says, in a kinder voice than he has ever had before. This is the voice of God.

"What a strange creature you've chosen for your voice," she says.

"Would you rather a burning bush?"

"I would prefer that you never destroy anything here, ever again."

He laughs. "It wouldn't hurt the bush to burn with my voice."

"Then, yes, I would have preferred that."

"I don't know. You have your bird and I have mine."

"Are you . . . making a joke?"

"Is that so surprising?"

Naamah eases her grip on Jael, and he moves up to her shoulder.

"Hello," Jael says.

"I'm sorry, Jael. I can't give you your voice here."

"Why not?" Naamah asks.

"I misspoke. I can give it to him, but I won't. It's not to be cruel," He says, knowing what Naamah's thinking. "It's in the hope that one day he'll return to where he belongs."

Naamah considers this, and then says, "Why are you here?"

"I wanted to speak with you."

"But you didn't want me to remember our talk."

"I didn't need you to, no."

"Well, say it, then."

"It's not an *it*. I don't have an order for you. A command. I want to talk."

Naamah laughs and starts to walk away.

"You're given a chance to talk to God and you walk away?"

She looks back at Him but keeps walking. "I'm drunk, God. If you just want to chat, come back another time." She laughs again.

"Do you not fear me, Naamah?"

"Do what you will," she says, turning her back on Him again, moving off into the dark. "Do what you will."

# TWENTY-FIVE

Their new home is close enough that, if they need to, they can empty their wagons and come back for more. But Naamah will never come back. She knows this as she sits in her wagon, holding the ropes, letting them hang, the slightest sagging arc down to the yoke that leads to the head of an ox.

Jael is on her shoulder, and now she is as mindful of him as he's always been of her.

She remembers more dreams than the ones with Jael—so many dreams that she is having trouble telling which happened and which didn't. In one, she is enjoying a field of neatly cut grass during a sunset, enjoying it so much that she lies down to sleep, and when she wakes she sees hundreds of small spiderwebs revealed by the dew, each droplet reflecting the grass back to itself, in an upside-down and curving world that could not exist. Even now she startles thinking of the life in the grass, but she can't place where that field might have been, how old she was, anything.

But the memory of talking with God is clear, even if there's hardly a reason to recall it. She finds herself going over every word in her head.

And as if she had called Him, the vulture returns with His kind voice: "Good morning."

Around them, though the wagons continue, her family looks smeared, slowing down through time. "I guess it would be foolish to ask if they are okay," she says.

He laughs, perched beside her.

She asks, "Won't the animals be discomforted by your presence?"

"Do you think they will? I could stop them as well, but I thought you'd want to continue your good pace."

Naamah finds it easier to talk to Him if she doesn't look at the vulture. "Yes, I would like us to reach the river by nightfall."

"Terrific. Let's continue our chat."

"I like your laugh," she blurts, as if the thought forced itself through her lips.

"You do. And you like how it comes out of the vulture's beak, that juxtaposition."

"Yes." And then she asks, "Do you cry?"

"If vultures cry, then yes."

"Don't you *know* if vultures cry?"

"I do. But I don't always take the time to remember." The vulture isn't moving at all, besides his mouth, but Naamah has the sense that an adolescent boy has taken his place. "Where would all the mystery be?" He says, leaning back and swinging His feet out.

"Is mystery something that matters to you?" Naamah asks.

"Yes. Don't you like mystery?"

"I'm not sure." Naamah focuses on the land as it slips past, under the ox's feet, but it unsettles her stomach. "And I didn't mean, do you cry when you speak through the vulture? I meant, do you cry, as the Lord?"

"Ah, well, that's another matter." The young man of Him is sitting upright again, feet tucked under the bench. "No, I don't." After a beat, He adds, "Would you like to know if vultures can cry?"

"I thought you didn't—"

"I tried not to, but I thought about it anyway." The vulture flaps his wings. "There's never been a vulture that has cried yet! Although they do have tear ducts, which could theoretically produce tears. One day one will get something stuck in its eye and it will cry profusely."

"Like one day, that's a possibility? Or like one day, for sure, you know it?"

"One day. I know it."

"What is it like, to experience time like that?"

"Tricky. Trying to figure out if that vulture cried before now or after."

Naamah laughs.

"What?"

"I didn't think you'd find anything tricky."

"Oh yes. Loads of stuff. Time, for one."

"What's another?"

"You're another."

"Me?"

"Mmm, you're very tricky. You verge on the absurd."

Naamah laughs a single laugh, like she was caught off guard.

"You want to know why," He says. "That's understandable. You're unpredictable. I honestly could not guess if you were going to choose to stay with the angel or with your family. I saw both paths clearly."

"You know about that, huh?"

"Naamah, the angel is a part of me."

"You mean—"

"Yes."

"I've had sex with you?" she says.

"No," He says.

"No."

"Do you want to have sex with me?"

"No!"

"It's okay if you do."

"I don't!" She shuffles a little away from the vulture.

"You couldn't even if you wanted to. Only with forms I could take on. And what would that be, anyway?"

"I'm not thinking about that, because I don't want to have sex with you."

"Okay, okay." He laughs. "What do you want to talk about?"

Naamah pushes a breath out. "You know what."

"The flood."

"Yes," she says.

"Bethel."

She looks at Him, looks into His vulture's eye. "Yes."

"She could have come onto the ark, Naamah. She didn't want to."

"No, she couldn't. Don't do that. She thought I would be punished if she came on the boat, in case it denied your word in some way."

"I went to her after that."

"What?" Naamah says, her eyes filling with tears.

"I let her know she could go to you. But she was ready, Naamah."

The tears roll down her cheeks and fall onto her thighs.

"I'm sorry. It was her decision."

Naamah shakes her head and yells, "Did you talk to *everyone* before talking to me?"

"You know I didn't."

"So why? Why come to me now? Do I have a decision to make? Some task to take on?" She pushes tears off her face with her fingers, moving fast and sloppy.

"No."

"No, I'm just the absurd woman."

"Naamah—"

"Leave! Leave now!" she yells, and then more calmly, "Come back again if you need to. But leave now."

He does.

NAAMAH HEARS DANIT CRYING. She looks over at Noah driving his wagon. He sees her flushed cheeks and he mouths, "Are you okay?"

She nods. She feels Jael on her shoulder. She looks around to each wagon, counting them. Adata is farthest ahead, and Naamah catches glimpses of her face. She wonders if Adata's lover was given the choice to come on the boat, if she chose to die instead. She wonders if Adata would have fallen in love with the angel and if she would have stayed with her underwater. And would the angel have loved her? Was there nothing about Naamah at all that the angel loved? Would any living woman have been enough? Maybe Naamah met people only in moments when they were susceptible to a difficult woman.

WHEN THEY REACH THE RIVER, it's late and dark. The light of the moon catches on the water and wet rocks. They look over it for a long time. They gather water. They talk about where they should settle, which side of the river, how far from the bank. Someone says the words *to avoid flooding*, and everyone feels it in their stomachs, the word *flood* sounding small, as if there were nothing remarkable about it.

A WEEK GOES BY. NAAMAH likes to stand at the river and look back on their tents. Four for their families, four for animals, and two more for storage. They have started building stables and fencing off fields, so the horses and oxen don't always have to be tethered. Their new village is expanding the way water flows through dirt, reaching this way and that.

Today, Naamah starts the garden, closer to the river, where the ground is ready for it. Jael is with her, scratching at the dirt. She creates row after row, tearing through the surface of the earth until it loosens. She sees how the earth gathers itself, tightens its skin, when no one is there to break it.

Naamah feels as raw as the dirt. But she's not sure what she's waiting for, what seed she could take right now, what she could grow to the point of blossoming.

———

IN ONE ROW OF DIRT she is forming, she comes across the bones of a hand. She digs above the bones of the wrist and finds the two longer bones of the forearm. She goes back to the tent of horses and cuts off some of a horse's mane and makes a brush with the hair and wood and twine. She collects more bone tools, more wood, and returns to the garden beds.

She digs up from the forearm and finds the upper arm, the shoulder; she uncovers the skull. Without looking at anything too closely, she continues, working down into the chest and the ribs. She doesn't dig deep enough to reach the spine but moves down to where the pelvis protrudes. Then she exposes the left leg, then the right. Then back to the shoulder, to work down through the right arm to the smallest finger bones.

She clears it of more dirt with a wooden spoon and then brushes the bones clean. The body rests like a relief in stone. Only upon seeing it entirely uncovered does Naamah understand that it's a child's remains.

"Dear one," Jael says.

Naamah lies down beside it, with her head near the skull, then sits up to see how far her legs continue beyond the thin, bony feet. She puts her hand on the child's hand.

The dead of the flood are gone. Naamah doesn't know how, but they are. This child died before the flood, which means there are other remains, which means that people lived here before. And of course they did. What a lovely river. What a bounty of life.

But Naamah had been fooled by the newness of the unflooded world. Now she realizes that her family, their new world, will live in communion with the old world, but not with the destruction that birthed one world from the other. As if that's a blessing.

SHE LIES BACK DOWN in the dirt. The neck of the child is so small. Naamah had never thought of her neck as a vulnerable part of her body until she let a man kiss her there. She wonders if a woman would have made her feel that way, if a woman had been her first kiss.

In their old desert, there once was a woman who sliced her own neck. Naamah hadn't known her, but the idea of any woman killing herself didn't surprise her. She didn't wonder if she could have helped her. She held on more closely to her intention to live a life she wanted to live.

But everything changed when God spoke to Noah. Her intention was overwhelmed. That didn't feel bad at first.

Naamah runs her finger over the exposed vertebrae of the child's neck. Even without the body, the skin, she recognizes the feeling from the necks of her boys when they were young.

She remembers hacking into an animal's bones for food, gripping them tight, sucking out the marrow, her hands still salty with blood from handling the kill.

These bones—she taps on the largest, in the child's leg—are hollow, have been hollow for a long time. Her fingernail holds the vibration of the bone, telling her which things in her life the bone is harder than, which softer. She closes her eyes.

———

NAAMAH WAKES WHEN SHE HEARS tapping, thinking it is Jael, but it is the vulture tapping on a bone.

"Get away!" she yells at him.

"You are burning, Naamah."

"What?"

"Your skin is burning."

She runs her hands over her face and it stings. "I fell asleep."

He feels no need to respond to something so evident. He takes a few steps into the torn dirt of the garden.

"Doesn't mean you should peck at this child's bones," she says.

"It's no longer a child."

She looks at his taloned feet in her garden, and even that feels like a trespass. "Where is Jael?"

"He went back to your little tents. Danit was crying."

"Why are you here?" she asks.

"He is coming. I was going to wait, but I saw you were burning."

She can't conceal her surprise. "Were you concerned for me, vulture?"

But before he can respond, God is there.

"Good afternoon, Naamah," He says warmly.

"Hello."

He steps out of the garden and then turns back to face it. "The plants will be bountiful, and the birds will eat their seeds and carry them all over the world."

"That's great," Naamah says, flatly.

"Yes, plant more than you'll need. I will see to it that the birds come."

"Okay."

He stops and looks at Naamah. "You're being short with me."

"I am," she says. She closes her eyes and a vaguely human shape is before her. It feels like a shadow. Someone standing too close.

"What are you doing?" He asks.

"It's just easier to talk to you like this. You're not God speaking through a vulture."

"What am I?"

"You look like a lanky teenage boy, in my head."

"Would you prefer I come to you like that?"

She tilts her head. "Could you?"

"Not here. Here, I'd have to speak through, well, the only people here. Come to you through Shem, let's say."

She doesn't open her eyes, but she points her head as if she's glaring at him and cuts her voice low. "Don't you dare."

He laughs. "I wouldn't. I wouldn't, okay?"

She relaxes again.

"I could come to you in a dream in any form you like."

"I don't think Sarai would let you."

He nods His vulture's head. "She is something."

"She is real, then?"

"She is."

"Does she know you?" Naamah asks.

"Not yet. But I think she will. She is becoming more and more godlike."

"Do you fear her?"

"I'm not sure I've ever experienced fear. How would you describe it?"

"Your heart races, or you let out a yell you can't help, or you start sweating."

"That's all physical."

"Oh, right." He waits patiently while she thinks. "Well, I guess it often happens when you're trapped in some way, so the feeling of fear is tied up with calculating escape. The thing you fear—is it something you can outrun? Can you fight it? If not, should you still fight it, get one good hit in and then run? If you're forced to surrender, then can you decide *not* to show fear?"

"This is how you felt with the tiger?"

She nods. "Except the questions were easy to answer because the tiger was stronger. I just tried not to be scared."

"But you did not understand that she was only being true to the animal she is. You did not forgive her. If you had accepted her, wouldn't your fear have dropped away?"

"Did I owe her that?"

He doesn't respond.

"Would you not have saved me?"

"No," He says.

"No?"

"You are an old woman, Naamah. As much waits for you in death as in life. You have done everything here that was needed of you and more."

"I did not do it for you."

"I know that. But I'm grateful nonetheless."

And then He is gone. The vulture returns, looks down at his feet in the hot, caked dirt, and moves back into the garden.

"Where is He?" she asks.

"He had to attend to another matter."

"And you, Metatron?" She can't hide her disdain for him. "Must you stay?"

He shits in her garden as he takes off into the sky, and she mixes it into the dirt.

NAAMAH RETURNS AS EVERYONE IS leading horses into the newly finished stables.

"How do they look, Mom?" Ham yells over to her.

"They look great!"

Noah is smiling. Jael is on his shoulder. He's beginning to see the life they will have here.

Naamah catches up with Neela, who's bringing up the end of the line, carrying Danit.

"Hello," Naamah says.

Neela nods at her. Things haven't been the same between them since the night Naamah took Danit to the water.

When the first horse is in the stall, Neela brings Danit's hand to its side and says, "Horse."

Danit is happy. She makes a gurgling sound high in her throat.

"Did you get burned out there today?" Neela asks. "You look red."

"I fell asleep in the sun. Is it bad?"

"Not too bad."

"It stings," Naamah says.

"Do you want some milk to put on it?"

"You don't mind?"

"No." Neela hands Danit to Naamah. It's the first time Naamah's held her since that night.

Neela takes out her breast and with one hand squeezes milk into the other. Then Neela puts her breast back and looks at the milk. "Want me to do it?" she asks.

"Okay," Naamah says.

Neela dips two fingers into her cupped left hand and runs them across Naamah's forehead. She dips them again, touches lightly at the center of Naamah's chin, then runs them along her jawline and over the tips of her ears. Then she rubs her hands together and takes Naamah's face in her hands, placing her thumbs on her nose and dragging them across her cheeks. Naamah hasn't been touched this way, this lightly, with such care, since her mother died.

"Thank you," she says.

"Sure."

Naamah holds Danit out toward Neela, but she doesn't take her back.

"Would you mind if I go bathe?" Neela asks.

"Take your time," Naamah says. But what she wants to do is drop down, kiss Neela's hands, and thank her for these first signs of forgiveness.

NAAMAH TAKES DANIT BACK TO a tent to play. Jael follows. Naamah lies down, placing Danit with her knees in the hay and her head and arms on Naamah's stomach. And then Danit does what all of her sons did: she pushes herself up, trying to raise her head. Jael is on the other side of Naamah's stomach, bouncing his head for Danit to see.

"Hello," he says.

And she smiles and her head plops back down. She smushes her nose into Naamah's belly, left and right. She sputters and drools.

Then she starts again, her neck looking perfectly strong for a moment, Naamah cheering her on.

# TWENTY–SIX

In a dream, God comes to her as the boy she imagines Him to be, tall and gangly, like her boys before they filled out, as if He might knock things over with His elbows, as if He must have a lot of bruises on His legs.

"How are you here?" she asks Him.

"After we last talked, I started thinking. I had slowed down, hoping Sarai would pass me. But when I realized that was an unconscious decision—perhaps made out of fear, you might say—well, then I reevaluated and sought her out."

"Did you kill her?"

"What? No! You do think terribly of me, don't you?"

"You are capable of terrible things."

"I am. I am that," He says. "But I am not terrible. If I had not created the new world, Sarai would never have been born, would never have birthed Isaac. You cannot see it, but I can."

"Will you interfere again?"

"Do you want me to?" He asks.

"No."

"Even if it were to help?"

"No."

"Many would not agree with you, Naamah. Do you speak for them?"

"No," she admits.

"Nor should you!" He brings Himself close to her face.

She thinks He is trying to threaten her, and in response to that alone, she kisses Him. Her tongue slides deep into His mouth.

"I don't think you even wanted to do that," He says, stepping back from her.

"How did we survive this long?" she asks.

"Your family?"

"Us, and you."

"I don't know," He says.

"I can tell you're tiring of me," Naamah says.

"I'm sorry."

"Don't be. In this way, you are the most human I have ever seen you."

Naamah wakes up as if she were pushed out of the dream. It's still dark out. She hears a boar shriek.

STILL ASLEEP, Noah says, "Is everything okay?"

She says, "I think I kissed God."

"How was it?" he asks.

"I couldn't feel it. I was dreaming."

"Not very good, then," he says.

She laughs into her throat.

NAAMAH CAN'T FALL BACK TO SLEEP. She wraps a blanket around herself and heads in the direction of the shriek. Soon she sees two wolves eating a boar. She hides behind a tree and watches them. She remembers both animals from the boat.

She feels a compulsion to help the boar even though it's already dead. She also feels pride for the wolves in their success. She feels relief that her family did not domesticate them.

The wolves had worked together to bring down the boar, but now they tug the carcass away from each other, breaking multiple ribs at once until a piece of flank comes free. They chew as if they're choking, moving the bones through their mouths, toward the back teeth, hanging their heads over the boar's body, claiming it. Eventually they fall quiet, still ripping apart the body, drawing stringy parts up to their mouths, but sated.

When they finish and leave, Naamah goes to the boar. She piles the pieces of its body onto her blanket. She drags the blanket to a dead tree and shoves each piece into the broken, hollowed trunk. She calls it a burial. And then she goes and washes herself and the blanket in the river.

MONTHS GO BY. The things that could be done are endless, but the things that need to be done are few. To feed themselves, to bathe themselves, to rest. Their lives here are simple.

Japheth decides to start mapping their surroundings, traveling out on a horse for days, coming back and recording everything on the canvas of his tent. Jael likes to travel with him, and Japheth seems taken with the bird as well.

Adata sleeps next to where he started the map. She traces the river with her finger. At their home, he's drawn a circle with a line down the center. Two halves. Soon Adata announces that she is pregnant. She puts her hand to her stomach, unsure of what is real.

IN THE DAYS after the announcement, Naamah can see that Sadie is upset. "Have you been trying, too?" Naamah asks her.

"Oh." Sadie blushes, upset. "Am I so obvious?"

"It's okay," Naamah says as she takes Sadie into her arms. "It will happen."

"I am disappointing Shem."

"No, you aren't."

"Yes, yes, I am. I know he notices when my blood comes. We don't even need to speak about it."

"Maybe you should."

"I would make a good mother."

"You will be a wonderful mother. I know that. Come on now." Naamah holds her closer, waiting for Sadie to signal, to fuss a shoulder. But she doesn't.

"What if God doesn't want me to have children?"

"God has nothing to do with it, Sadie."

"Of course He does." Now Sadie pulls away. "You put us all at risk by not believing in Him."

"I believe in Him. How could I not after what we've seen?"

"You know what I mean."

"I don't think our faith in Him should determine how we live our lives." She takes Sadie's hand, but Sadie pulls that away, too.

"Until you accept Him, we will all be punished, all around you. Maybe I am just the first." She moves away from Naamah.

"Sadie, please."

Sadie walks off in the direction of the newly fenced-off field of goats, some of whom have had kids. Past them are the hutches of rabbits, who have multiplied so quickly. Everywhere Sadie goes, she will be surrounded by flourishing.

NAAMAH IS SOAKING in a hot spring when the vulture comes to her again, already carrying the voice of God.

"I didn't like our last conversation," He says.

"Then why come talk to me again?"

"Are you not worried by what Sadie said?"

"No. It can take a long time to get pregnant. It's not uncommon, and neither is being upset by it."

"I could keep it from taking a long time."

"I know that." Naamah is angry. "But you chose her for this." She stands up, out of the water, her brown body shining brilliantly in the sun. "She will get pregnant. She will have countless children. And if she were not to, that would punish you, not me."

"Yet you are upset, too."

"If she were never to get pregnant, I would help her find happiness in her life."

"You would help her abandon her faith." His voice begins to boom louder than His vulture body should allow.

"If she chose to wrap up her faith in her fertility, then yes!"

His vulture's eyes begin to turn white, and He raises His wings. "Why shouldn't I punish you, Naamah?"

"My life or death means nothing now!"

He calms down. His eyes turn brown once more in His vulture's yellow head. "Do you provoke me intentionally?" He asks.

Naamah slouches back into the water. "Yes. I've never seen you outside of these ridiculous bodies."

And then, louder than anything Naamah has ever heard before, He shouts, "If you want to see me, see me." He spreads His wings to block the sky, and everything is replaced with blackness unlike anything she could imagine. She lifts her hands out of the water, feels the air catching on her fingers, hears the water drip from them, but all she sees is black. Then His voice speaks again.

"Anything that comes from the blackness is a creation. Nothing can be born of light because light *is* already. But from me can come all things. From me can come a world the likes of which you cannot fathom because when you came out of the blackness you had not the power to fathom it. Blame me not for your limitations, Naamah, but take with you what I offer."

Though Naamah can see nothing, she closes her eyes. She turns her body, crosses her arms over the edge of the hot spring, and buries her head in them. In this one position she has experienced darkness close to this, her own thick flesh canceling the light.

"Is this not what you wanted?" the voice continues. "Look upon me, Naamah."

Her body is lifted out of the springs, her face forced out of her arms, her eyes opened.

"Am I not deserving of your love?"

He casts her onto the ground. A cloud of dirt rises around her, and she coughs until it settles. When she opens her eyes, He is gone, and a layer of dirt covers every inch of her. She walks weakly to the river and wades in, until the cold water is over her head, and then she swims for the first time since the days she swam from the boat.

She swims until everything hurts. She swims until she has the choice to die in the water, if only she should stop. And then, when she's sure she doesn't want to die, she swims back to the river's bed.

NOAH FINDS NAAMAH COLLAPSED BY the river. He picks her up onto his shoulder and carries her home, puts her into bed. On her third day of sleep, Jael returns from a trip with Japheth. Jael sits beside her, takes her finger in his beak. Japheth asks if there's anything he can do, but Noah turns him away. He turns everyone away as Naamah's sleep continues. And as the days pass, even he begins to leave her, to spend his days as he might if she were gone, if she had never been.

IN HIS OWN TENT, Japheth draws a lake he's discovered—the angel's lake. He has walked all around it, and now, on the canvas, he marks its length in steps. Adata touches the new lake. Japheth tells her of the wildflowers already beginning to grow there, the sight of the mountains around it. She revels in the new stories he brings, and he touches her stomach.

"When do you think I will be able to feel the baby kick?" he asks.

"I don't know," she says. "You could ask Ham when he felt Danit."

"Do you feel it kicking?"

She smiles. "Yes."

He kisses her. "Should I be worried about my mother, do you think?"

"Not yet," she says.


JAEL GOES TO SLEEP beside Naamah. In his dream he is perched in a rain forest he remembers, and there she is.

"Are you okay?" he asks. "This doesn't look like one of your dreams."

"It's your dream this time," she says. "This is where you lived before the flood."

"It's beautiful."

"It is," she says.

"What happened to you?"

"God showed Himself to me. And I decided to live. I don't remember more than that."

"Will you wake up?"

"I think so."

"Noah is worried about you."

"Not my children?"

"No," he says.

"We have trained them to find nothing unusual."

Jael nods.

"Will you come back here, do you think?"

Jael looks around. He shuffles to the left on the branch. "When you are well."

"I will miss you."

"Won't we still see each other in our dreams?"

"Maybe."

"I won't go unless we will. Promise me."

"Okay," she says, "I promise."

"You can't promise it, I know. Even I know that."

"You're right, but it felt good to say it."

"Yeah? All right, me too." He thinks for a second before yelling, "I promise you all the fish you can eat!"

Naamah laughs. "I promise you all the seeds you can eat!"

"I promise you the best sunsets!"

"I promise you the best days!"

"I promise you love and happiness!"

"I—" She gathers him up in her arms.

"It does feel good to say it," he says.

"It does," she says, beginning to cry.

"You should wake up, Naamah."

"I should," she says. She looks at her own body in the branches of the forest, shafts of light breaking through the canopy. She catches sight of a skink on the floor of the forest. She wonders when she will see an animal and not remember the ways in which she cared for it.

## TWENTY–SEVEN

When Jael wakes, Naamah is still asleep, but her breath is steady, and she does not sweat, and she is not pale. All is well—she's just asleep.

The rest of them carry on with their lives, which means that even the dread around the prospect of Naamah's death is something they can become accustomed to. In her absence, they tend her garden. Jael continues to visit her in his dreams. Japheth starts going out again on his horse. The map grows larger in the tent. Adata's stomach grows larger, too. For the first time, Danit laughs at a face that Ham makes. Neela starts to paint again.

The birds come as God said they would. Sadie sees them first and yells until everyone is out of their tents. Together they follow the dark sheet of birds to the garden. The sun comes through gaps in their formation like sparks.

When the birds land, the ground can't be seen. They peck and peck. And when they leave again, the noise of their shuffling wings is tremendous. Neela covers Danit's ears. Everything falls quiet again as the birds fly higher, as they catch the currents of air.

WEEKS LATER, STILL ASLEEP, Naamah is lying in the tree in the rain forest again when Sarai comes to her. "Am I dying?" Naamah asks her.

"No," she says. "You saw God. Your body needs to rest."

"Don't I need to eat? Drink water?"

Sarai smiles. "No. Your body has been forced into a kind of hibernation in order to recover. Everything has slowed."

"How are you? I heard God spoke to you."

Sarai reaches behind her neck and gathers her long black hair, which is down now but still plaited and studded with gold. She pulls it over her shoulder and lies back on a branch. The two women, lounging there, look like the world was made for them. Their bodies dappled, their bodies round and soft, the tissue of their breasts resting to the sides of their rib cages, their arms strong, their legs stronger, their heads the most peculiar things in the rain forest.

"Did He tell you that?" asks Sarai.

"Yes."

"Speaking to Him is not like speaking to you. It's as if He forgets I was human."

"Are you not human anymore?"

"Decidedly not."

Naamah raises herself up on her right elbow and her breasts fall to the right. If Sarai isn't human anymore, perhaps she isn't either.

Perhaps in another place, she could look upon her body and know what new thing she is becoming.

IN ANOTHER DREAM, Naamah asks Sarai to take her to the strangest place she's ever been.

Sarai takes them to a beach of white sand and says, "It looks like a cloud was cursed and turned to stone."

"Every cloud," Naamah says.

"No! Wait!" Sarai yells. And then they are at a lake that's red.

"Can I touch it?" Naamah asks.

Sarai looks at her. "You're dreaming, Naamah. You can do whatever you want."

Naamah puts her hand under the surface of the water and looks at it, in perfect stillness. "Can nothing hurt me in the dream?"

"I don't think so."

Naamah's hand fades to nothing, and she thinks, *After all this, am I only becoming a ghost?*

"You're waking up," Sarai says.

Naamah's whole body is gone now, but she can still hear Sarai.

"If I don't see you again," Sarai says, "it was good to see you."

IN THE TENT, Naamah feels her mouth first. She can feel that it tastes bad, smells bad. Her tongue is thick and stiff, and when she opens her mouth, she takes a breath in like a gasp, straight to her belly. She coughs. She opens her eyes.

"Hello," says Jael.

She can't speak yet, but she smiles. She moves her tongue around her mouth. She feels the two lines carved into her tooth. She was already beginning to forget them before she fell asleep. Everything she can do to her body, her body can absorb.

Jael flies off and returns with Noah. She tries to sit up, but when she can't, Noah lifts her, and she rests her head on him.

"I have water. Do you want to try to drink?" he asks.

She nods into his shoulder. He leans her back and holds a bag of water to her lips and tilts it up. Swallowing the water hurts, but she does it.

"I can get you some broth. Do you want to eat?"

She nods again, so he lays her back down, gets a bowl of broth, and brings it back. He places it on the ground and looks for something to prop her up. Jael flies around the tent as if he's helping. Soon she's propped up, and Noah is spooning broth to her lips and she's drinking it down. But Jael doesn't stop flying around the top of the tent, chirping and whistling, making every sound he can make.


NAAMAH REGAINS HER STRENGTH. She takes it slow. The sun seems too bright, but every day it gets more tolerable as she forgets the depths that God showed her.

Soon she's strong enough to watch Danit, and Neela leaves Danit with her constantly. Danit crawls around Naamah's feet as Naamah practices standing. She shifts her weight from one foot to another.

Naamah says to Danit, "Maybe I should be down there with you, huh?"

Naamah sits, and then leans forward until her palms hit the ground. She rocks back and forth until she can get up on her knees. She moves ahead her left knee, her right hand, and then her right knee and left hand.

"No. No, no. This is worse." She laughs.

Danit laughs back.

Naamah crawls her arms out until she can fall to her side. "What do you think? How much longer will I be like this?"

Danit climbs up on her until she's standing. She whacks one hand on Naamah's shoulder. She bends her knee and her body dips and she loses her balance and she falls back onto her butt. She looks at Naamah as if the ground has offended her.

"Oh, baby, it happens," Naamah says.

Danit cries, and it could be for any number of reasons.


ADATA COMES BACK TO HER tent one day to find Danit and Naamah there. Japheth's map has extended to the highest point of the tent, and Naamah's lying in the middle of it all, looking up, dictating to Danit, *a river, a mountain, a lake.*

Adata doesn't make a sound.

"And where there is nothing marked, that is the desert," Naamah is saying.

Danit spots Adata and crawls over to her. Naamah cranes her neck to make sure Danit isn't leaving the tent.

"Adata!" she says.

"Hi, Naamah."

"I hope it's okay that we're in here."

Adata comes over to her. "It is," she says. She sits down with her stomach large in her lap.

Naamah puts her hand, palm up, on Adata's leg, and Adata holds it. "How are you doing?" Naamah asks.

"I'm good. Tired."

Danit crawls over to them and touches Adata's belly.

"Baby," Adata says.

Naamah looks back at the map.

Adata asks, "What happened to you?"

"I don't know," Naamah says, because that's what she's been saying to everyone.

"You know," Adata says.

Naamah looks at her. "Why do you want to know?"

Adata shakes her head.

"What is it?"

"Are we in danger, Naamah?"

"No. I would have told you that. We wouldn't still be here."

"So nothing did this to you?"

"Nothing you need to worry about."

"See! You're doing it again. It was *something* that did this to you, but you think none of us need to fear it. How can you know that?"

"I know it because if He wanted to harm you, He would already have done it. His intentions aren't hidden."

"God did that to you?"

"I don't think He knew the effect it would have. I don't think He—"

"No. Stop. Just stop," Adata says, and she gets up and starts to leave the tent.

"He's not what you think He is," Naamah says.

Adata spins around. "He has to be!" She puts her hands in her hair and takes them out again. "He has to be because that's why I've accepted all of this!"

"*I'm* glad you're here."

"That doesn't mean enough, Naamah. Not for me."

"Yes, it does."

"I should've died in that flood," Adata says.

"No, you—"

"You should have, too. He could have started again."

"Maybe, but we made it easier for Him by caring for all of the animals."

"I'm not solely a caretaker, Naamah."

"Not to me."

"To Him?"

"I don't speak for Him."

Adata starts to leave again and Danit follows her.

"Adata," Naamah says. "Danit."

"I've got her," Adata says over her shoulder.

Naamah stays, looking at the marks Japheth has made in the tent. Soon he will have mapped out everything he can reach with a horse with the intention of returning. But with a project such as this, he will not be content to stop. When he proposes to Adata that they move on from here, Naamah imagines she will agree to it.

THE NEXT WEEK, it rains so much one night that it reminds everyone of the flood, even if only in their sleep. In the morning, the river has flooded. Tops of bushes look like they're sitting on top of the water, and Naamah is reminded of the heads of the dead children as she looks out across it.

Neela comes up next to her. "Will you sit for me, Naamah? For a painting?"

"You want to paint me? Why?"

"Honestly? We thought you were going to die, Naamah. I thought we would lose Noah, too, if you died. And I want something *of* you, if that makes sense."

Naamah looks at the river, whose boundaries were never boundaries, whose water was never its own, just a collection of water cutting a path. Should the water be named *river* if it's only that? Should it be named at all?

"I will sit for you," she says.


Every day Neela paints her. Naamah has never been so still in her life. She sits cross-legged in the dirt, and she tries to enjoy the hours. She focuses on the warmth of the dirt on her legs, the sunlight on her arms. Some days Jael sits with her.

"Do you want me to paint Jael, too?" Neela asks.

"Whatever you want," Naamah says.

Every evening Neela insists that Naamah returns home before she returns with the painting. After Naamah passes her, she turns the painting from the direction of the tents.

"I won't look," Naamah says, raising her hands in the air.

"Let me have my fun, won't you?" And Neela smiles.

# Naamah

———

AT LAST SADIE IS PREGNANT. With her pregnancy, her great joy returns. Neela is done with her painting, but she hides it away so that Sadie can be the center of attention for a few days.

In secret, Naamah weaves a giant wreath together from branches she's collected. She asks everyone to pick wildflowers and bring them to her tent. She has them each tuck the long stems into the frame of the wreath.

Early one morning, after Sadie goes to wash in the river, Naamah and Shem carry the wreath into their tent.

"Do you think she'll like it?" Naamah asks.

"She's going to love it," Shem says. "It's great, Mom."

Naamah puts her arm around him. "I'm so excited for you."

"Me too," he says.

"Do you like it here?"

"I do," he says.

She smiles as she steps away from him. "I better go before she comes back."

"You don't want to be here when she sees it?"

She shakes her head and walks out into the sunlight. The day has come on strong and hot.


WHEN NEELA DOES REVEAL HER painting, the family applauds. It looks just like Naamah. It reminds Naamah she is, in and of her body, a forgettable woman. Beautiful, but forgettable. And though that is a feeling she often yearns for, to be confronted with it like this makes her feel like she might die. She wonders if God guided Neela's hand to capture her this way. She wonders if she might turn around and see the Metatron there, smirking, as much as a vulture can smirk.

THE NEXT MORNING JAEL IS GONE. At first she thinks he might be with someone else, but then she puts her fingers through her hair and feels a spot on her scalp that stings—a small scratch like when they first met. She remembers what he said in their last dream, that he would leave when she was well, and she thinks, *Is this well?*

She finds Japheth scraping a hide clean.

"When are you leaving again?" she asks.

"Soon."

"I bet you'd like to follow Jael wherever he is right now, the way he followed you."

He stops working on the hide. "Jael left?"

She nods.

He returns to her question. "Wouldn't anyone?" he says.

"I don't think so. I think most of us like the home we're making here."

"The world is nearly empty right now. It will never be that way again. I think I have to see it."

"And what about being a father?"

"I can do that, too."

"Okay," she says.

"You don't think I can."

"I do. If you say you can, then you can." But she wonders if Japheth will feel the same way about exploring the world after he holds his child. And as the child gets older, when the child is so in love with Adata, and they seem to delight in each other and their home—won't he want to be a part of that?

Or maybe he will always be outside of it. Maybe he has inherited that part of Naamah and will build it out to an extreme. Maybe the wonders of the world will be enough. Maybe he will stand behind a waterfall or at the edge of a canyon and his laugh will be so loud and true that the world will split in two at his mirth and that will make even more places for him to explore.

NEXT SHE FINDS Noah collecting eggs from the hens.

"Jael is gone," she says.

He stops. "I'm sorry, Naamah. I know you love him."

She reaches her hand into a nest and finds two warm eggs. She places them into his basket. "I do," she says.

He lowers his head next to her and kisses her cheek.

She takes a big breath and keeps her head straight. She knows if she looks at him she'll cry, and he knows it, too.

He goes back to the hens.

"I'll be at the river, then," she says, and she walks off as if someone might scold her for being late.

SHE SITS WITH HER FEET in the pool of the hot spring. She reaches to touch the white crust that's beginning to cover the rocks beside it, where the water rushes over and evaporates off, leaving its minerals behind. How thick the crust must have been before the flood. And how fully it might return. And how did the geyser understand the flood? And how did the geyser understand the dead? And how does the geyser understand Naamah?

She steps back out of the pool, takes her sharpened bone, and chips away at the crust on the rocks, hacks away at it. Enough to leave a deep mark and change its shape. Enough that she's covered in sweat. And she promises herself that she'll return and do it over and over again.

If she is the bearer of this new world, then let everything be touched by her hand.

# ACKNOWLEDGMENTS

My partner, *my* Noah, made me feel this book was possible every time it felt impossible. He is my first reader and one of my two great loves. My other great love is our son, who inspires me every day, who pushes me to be kind and silly above all else.

Eleanor Stanford and Rachel Mennies read the book as I wrote it and helped me see the kind of book it could be. Catie Rosemurgy, Linda Gallant Moore, and Lynne Beckenstein cheered me on every step of the way. I could not have written it without them.

I also have to thank these amazing people: Sandy and Bob Schoenholtz, Rosser Lomax, Natalie Shapero, Sarah Einstein, Stephanie King, Denise Grollmus, Nicky Arscott, Dawn Lonsinger, Tracey Levine, Mariel Capanna, Stephanie Feldman, Nadine Darling, Cecily Wong, Vicki Lame, Cathy Day, and Ayşe Altinok. They supported me in too many different ways to list.

And thank you to my family: Mom (who reads everything I write), Dad, Nick, Vic, Bian, and Kiet. I'm nothing without all of you.

My agent, Sarah Yake, understood instantly how this book could exist outside of me. Her belief and encouragement meant and continues to mean the world to me.

My editor, Cal Morgan, made me admit to myself that this book will be read, and the next draft soared into a version I never could have imagined.

## Acknowledgments

And I never imagined that I could even ask for this type of support and vision for my work. I am eternally grateful to Sarah, Cal, the team at Riverhead Books (including Geoffrey Kloske, Jynne Dilling Martin, Kate Stark, Carla Bruce-Eddings, Michelle Koufopoulos, and Liza Sweeney), and the teams abroad.

Thank you to everyone who brings Naamah to the world.